Because "I AM"

Maribel Del Valle-Berdiel

Table Of Content

Dedication

To God, whose divine presence has been my constant companion. His grace has not only surrounded me but has carried me when I could not take another step on my own. His voice has whispered hope into the silence of despair, and His mercy has renewed my strength time and time again. Without Him, none of this would be possible, and because of Him, I can stand firm in faith. Thank you, Jesus!

To my children, Ninamarie, Victor, Kenneth, Angel Skye, and grandchildren Avian and Anthony, and to my fur baby, Buddy, whose laughter fills my heart with joy and whose lives are my daily reminder of purpose. You are the reason I keep moving forward, the living proof that love and grace can change the world. Your presence reminds me that I am never alone, for I carry you in every step of my journey. This book belongs to you as much as it belongs to me, for you are the heartbeat behind every word written here.

To my dear family & friends, each of you has been a living testament to the meaning of unwavering love. You have walked with me through laughter that brightened even the heaviest of days, through tears that felt unending, and through seasons of both joy and heartbreak. Your encouragement has been the steady flame that reminded me that even in darkness, light can still be found. I am grateful for the way you have shaped me, challenged me, and stood with me in ways words could never fully capture.

In loving memory of my grandparents, Angel & Josefine Placeres, whose wisdom and prayers left an indelible mark on my heart. They taught me to honor faith, to value prayer, and to trust God's timing even when I did not understand it. Their lives were lessons in quiet strength, in enduring love, and in the kind of faith that does not waver with circumstance. The seeds they planted in me continue to bloom, even now. Our home at 881 Madison Avenue is always a safe place, even in my dreams, that is where I always end up! Thankful for the journey that began on Madison Ave.

To my mentor/friend/sister in Christ, Maria Lugo, and my therapist, Shani Cephas. I know God placed you in my life for a reason, and I'm eternally grateful for your compassion and guidance.

My lifelong mentor and friends, Luis & Francy Lopez, thank you for believing in me when I didn't have the strength to do so myself! You've always spoken positivity into my life. You are the sweetest gifts I've ever received from God!

To my Uncles and Aunt who helped raise me and have always poured true love into me, Edwin, Ricky, Albert, Papo, and Titi Emily. They are pillars of love in my life!

To my sister, Emily, I will always love you near or far! When I think of you, it always brings me home to a place that only belongs to you and I!

To my Mom and Dad, Gladys Josaites and Felipe Del Valle, who love me unconditionally, your love and laughter have always kept me rising and grounded in this tough world. I find acceptance and grace!

To my BFFs Jeannette and Jessie, what a journey we've had. I'm so glad we've gotten through it and are still finding ways to dance in the rain. Love you.

My small circle of women prayer warriors, you know who you are! Iron sharpens iron. I'm so blessed by you!

To my husband Cholo, thank you for loving me as I am! Thank you for the journey and the safe place I've found in you! I will always love you!

Can't forget my grammar school teacher, Mrs. Healy, what an example of a heart that loves with no agenda, a heart that guides with consistency! Til this day, when I think of you, I know someone cared.

So much love for all these people!

And finally, to those unnamed souls who have walked briefly through my life — the mentors, teachers, neighbors, and strangers whose small acts of kindness or words of wisdom gave me courage in unseen moments. Though you may not know it, your presence touched my story, and for that, I dedicate this work in gratitude.

Prologue

The journey of faith is not always smooth. It rarely follows a straight path, free of obstacles or detours. More often than not, it is in the valleys — in the seasons of brokenness, silence, and waiting — that our faith is tested and deepened. Pain has a way of stripping us bare, taking away the comforts and securities we once clung to, and forcing us to confront our own weakness. Yet it is in these very moments of emptiness that the presence of God reveals itself most profoundly.

When I look back on the chapters of my life, I see a thread of God's grace running through each one. There were days when the weight of sorrow felt unbearable, when the walls seemed to close in, and when all hope appeared lost. There were moments of betrayal and disappointment that cut deeply, and losses that left scars I thought would never heal. But alongside the grief was a steady current of mercy — a presence that never let me drown, no matter how overwhelming the waters became.

This book was born from those experiences. It is not simply a record of trials and triumphs, but a testimony to the God who carried me through each one. My story is not unique in its hardships — pain and struggle touch every human life. What makes the difference is what we choose to do with that pain, and more importantly, what God chooses to do with us in the midst of it.

At the center of everything is the truth of God's eternal presence. When He spoke to Moses through the burning bush in the wilderness, His words carried power beyond comprehension: *"I AM WHO I AM"* (Exodus 3:14). This declaration was more than a name; it was a revelation of His nature — eternal, unchanging, ever-present. Generations later, those words still echo, reminding us that the God who was with Moses is the same God who is with us today.

For me, the phrase *"Because I AM"* became an anchor in the storms of life. It explained how I was able to take another step when everything inside me screamed to give up. It was the reason I could find hope when circumstances looked hopeless. Because God is "I AM" — sovereign, faithful, and unchanging — my story was never truly in my hands, but in His.

When I walked through seasons of grief and trauma, when the nights seemed endless and the silence deafening, this truth became the lifeline I clung to. God was not absent, though I often felt alone. He was there in the storm, whispering peace to my anxious heart. He was there in the waiting, teaching me patience and trust. He was there in my weakness, proving that His strength is perfected when we have none of our own.

Scripture confirmed what my soul was slowly learning. Psalm 91:11 promises, *"For He will command His angels concerning you to guard you in all your ways."* I have seen this promise unfold in my own journey. There were moments when I should have fallen apart, yet somehow I stood. There were times when despair should have crushed me, yet I found myself lifted by an unseen strength. I believe with all my heart that God's angels encamped around me in those seasons, protecting me in ways I will never fully understand.

This book is a reflection of that peace — the kind of peace that defies logic and circumstance. It is not a peace found in the absence of hardship, but in the assurance that hardship does not have the final word. It is the peace that comes when you realize you are never truly alone, that every tear shed is seen by God, and every prayer whispered is heard.

If you take nothing else from these pages, let it be this: your pain is not wasted. God is not indifferent to your suffering, nor is He distant from your struggles. Every experience, every heartbreak, every trial holds a place in the greater design He has written for your life. His plan is not always clear in the moment, and often it feels hidden behind the fog of grief, but it is always at work.

There is purpose in your story — even in the chapters you wish you could erase. God can use the broken pieces of your life to build something beautiful, something that not only transforms you but touches others in ways you may never fully realize.

This prologue is not simply an introduction to a book; it is an invitation. An invitation to step into my story, to walk alongside me through the valleys and mountaintops, and to discover, perhaps even within your own journey, that God has never left you. He is still "I AM." He always has been. And He always will be.

Chapter 1

Introduction

Because "I AM"

I wanted to be of service. The desire was strong, though I didn't really know what that would look like in practice. Sometimes, I even questioned whether I was truly capable of serving in the way I felt called to. I would pray and ask God for some kind of sign, something clear enough to reassure me that the longing I carried in my heart wasn't just wishful thinking.

To be honest, the thought of me writing a book felt like one of those BIG, BOLD prayer requests—an almost unreachable dream, something so far outside my comfort zone that it seemed nearly impossible. I wrestled with doubt. I didn't believe I had what it took. I struggled with confidence and kept asking myself how someone like me, someone so ordinary and unqualified by the world's standards, could possibly take on such a monumental task.

Yet, in spite of my doubts, I took a small step of faith. I prayed. I asked God, "If this is truly what You want me to do, then please, confirm it. Choose someone to deliver the message so I'll know it's from You." After that prayer, I released it into His hands.

Days turned into weeks, and weeks began to feel long. Nothing happened. No flashes of lightning, no voice from heaven. Just silence. But then, out of nowhere, God began to move in a way I never expected.

One afternoon, a close friend came by to visit. At that point, I hadn't shared with anyone my private dream of writing a book—not even her. I carried it quietly in my heart, unsure of how it would sound if spoken out loud. That evening, we sat together talking late into the night. In the middle of our conversation, she casually mentioned that her cousin was in the process of writing a book. My heart skipped. For a moment, excitement bubbled up inside me, but fear kept me silent. I didn't dare reveal my secret hope. I tucked it away again, too unsure of myself, too afraid of being vulnerable.

About a week later, we were chatting again, this time about something she had posted on Instagram. Suddenly, she turned to me, looked straight at me, and said, "Mari, you should write a book! You're really good with words!"

BAM. That was it. A spark ignited in my spirit. Her words, so simple yet perfectly timed, struck me as God's direct answer to my prayer. I felt my whole body light up inside. I knew in that instant it wasn't random—it was divine. God had heard me, and in His infinite wisdom, He chose the perfect messenger to deliver what I had been waiting for. It was His way of saying, "I see you. I hear you. This is your confirmation."

That moment gave me courage. It reminded me that God knows us better than we know ourselves. He knows what will reach us, how to speak to our hearts, and how to strengthen us when we falter. I walked away from that conversation feeling encouraged, seen, and empowered.

Still, as the days moved forward, I found myself asking practical questions. How would I even begin? I had no experience as a writer. I didn't know how to structure chapters or how to put my thoughts into a book that would speak to others. Yet deep inside, a steady voice reminded me that it wasn't about what I could do on my own. It was about what God could do through me. This wasn't about my ability but His. Not my timeline but His.

That truth settled in my heart. I decided I couldn't wait until I had everything figured out. I needed to start serving Him today, in this moment, with what I had and who I was.

James 2:17 tells us, "In the same way, faith by itself, if it is not accompanied by action, is dead." I realized then that I couldn't just pray and believe. I needed to move. I had to take action. And so here I am—a simple girl from Joyzie—not just sharing my story, but stepping into the greater story God has written for me from long before time began. He exists outside of Time, and His story for each of us has already been written into eternity.

One of the hardest parts in those early days was deciding on the title of the book. For months, I struggled. I wanted the title to carry the weight of what God had placed in my heart. I didn't want it to point to me. I wanted it to reflect Him—His grace, His plan, His glory. I longed for the title to remind people that their lives, too, are carefully and intentionally orchestrated by God.

Then one day, as I was driving two hours to visit my daughter and grandkids, the answer came in the most unexpected way. I happened to glance at the car in front of me, and its license plate read: *I AM 316.*

In that instant, my heart raced. "I AM." Those words carried me straight to Scripture. In Exodus 3:14, God speaks to Moses through the burning bush and says, "I AM WHO I AM. This is what you are to say to the Israelites: 'I AM has sent me to you.'" It was as if heaven opened up on that drive. I knew immediately that God was speaking to me again. That plate wasn't just a coincidence—it was a divine appointment.

God wasn't just confirming my calling to write; He was reminding me of who He is—the great *I AM.* Eternal. Unchanging. Present in every moment.

That same truth echoes in John 8:58, when Jesus declares, "Very truly I tell you, before Abraham was born, I am!" The message was clear: my journey wasn't about me. It was about Him, the Alpha and the Omega, the beginning and the end.

Interestingly, just a week before seeing that license plate, I had shared with a few friends the very significance of "I AM." I had told them that each time we introduce ourselves—"I am Maribel," "I am

John"—we are echoing God's name, the name He gave to Moses. With those two words, He goes before us.

And then, almost as if to seal the message, a week later I'm driving along and see "I AM 316." My spirit leapt. This was no accident. It was God weaving together a perfect confirmation of His plan.

It wasn't only a sign to me. It was a declaration: He is the author of this story. He is the One who called me. And He is the One who will see it through.

There have been countless ways that God has chosen to speak to me throughout my life. Sometimes His messages have come softly, in a whisper I did not recognize, and I'm sure I've missed them because I wasn't paying enough attention. Other times, His presence was undeniable—so clear, so powerful—that I couldn't help but stop and listen. Those moments became anchors for me, strengthening my faith and reminding me that I was never walking alone.

Proverbs 3:5-6 says, *"Trust in the Lord with all your heart and lean not on your own understanding; in all your ways submit to him, and he will make your paths straight."* That scripture has carried me through many seasons. Trusting in God has often meant surrendering my own understanding and letting go of the plans I carefully tried to hold together. It required me to say, "God, I don't know how this will turn out, but I trust You anyway." That surrender was not always easy, but it was always necessary.

Looking back over the years, I can see His hand at work—how God opened doors where none seemed to exist, how He guided me away from harm I didn't even see coming, how He provided strength when I had none of my own. He knew me better than I knew myself. And in those times when I thought I had been abandoned, I later discovered He was there all along, shaping the outcome with a wisdom far greater than mine.

Romans 8:28 reminds us, *"And we know that in all things God works for the good of those who love him, who have been called according to his purpose."* I hold onto that promise. Even in the confusing seasons, the heartbreaks, and the disappointments, God was weaving something meaningful. What I once saw as scattered pieces, I now see as part of His greater design. Every moment, even the painful ones, had purpose.

I have often wondered about the way God gives each of us our gifts—how He carefully places within us talents and abilities, shaping our paths before we even realize it. Some gifts are loud and visible, like a voice that commands attention or a talent that draws crowds. Others are quiet, almost hidden, but no less powerful: the ability to comfort, to listen, to create peace where there was chaos. If you've ever found yourself questioning your own gifts, wondering if they matter, I want you to know—I understand. You're not alone in that wondering.

For me, one of those gifts showed itself early. Since childhood, I have dreamed vividly—every night, almost without fail. At first, I thought everyone dreamed this way, with images so sharp and details so alive they seemed more like memories than imagination. But I soon realized that was not the case. My dreams were different, sometimes unsettling, often strikingly clear. I'm not a medium or a psychic, but I do believe this ability was placed in me by God. Over the years, certain dreams carried weight and meaning too strong to ignore. Some stirred me to prayer. Others prepared me for things I didn't yet understand.

Joel 2:28 speaks to this truth: *"And afterward, I will pour out my Spirit on all people. Your sons and daughters will prophesy, your old men will dream dreams, your young men will see visions."* I believe God still moves this way, still whispers through visions, dreams, and moments of divine inspiration. He has not grown silent—His Spirit continues to speak, if only we are willing to listen.

Growing up, I was especially close to my grandparents, who played a central role in raising me. My grandmother, in particular, carried her own gift for dreams and visions. Because of that, she never doubted me when I shared mine. I remember one dream in particular that has stayed with me all these years. In it, I saw a staircase stretching upward, beginning from her bedroom and rising all the way down Madison

Avenue. Above it, the sky was bright and filled with a deep blue light. At the top stood Jesus, His arms outstretched in welcome. Beneath us, the streets lay covered in white snow, glistening as though heaven itself had touched the earth.

When I told my grandmother about this dream, she didn't brush it aside. She smiled, her voice calm and steady, and told me, *"Don't worry, something beautiful is coming."* At the time, I didn't fully understand what she meant, but her words sank deep into my spirit.

Psalm 16:11 says, *"You make known to me the path of life; you will fill me with joy in your presence, with eternal pleasures at your right hand."* That dream, I later realized, was God preparing me, showing me a glimpse of what was to come—not in the way I expected, but in the way I would most need it.

On December 12, 1996, my phone rang with urgency. My uncle's frantic voice told me my grandmother was being rushed to the hospital. A heavy snowstorm had settled over the city, slowing everything down, but I drove as quickly as I could, my heart pounding with dread. By the time I arrived, paramedics were working on her, their hands moving rhythmically as they performed CPR. They let me ride with her in the ambulance, and as I sat there, fear pressing against my chest, that dream returned in a flash—the staircase, the snow, the image of Jesus waiting with open arms.

And then, as clearly as if she were sitting beside me, I heard my grandmother's voice again: *"Something beautiful is coming."* My heart broke at those words, because deep down, I understood what they meant. Seven days later, on December 19—just one day after her birthday—my grandmother passed away.

Revelation 21:4 gave me comfort in that time of grief: *"He will wipe every tear from their eyes. There will be no more death or mourning or crying or pain, for the old order of things has passed away."* Those words carried me when my own strength was gone. I believe with all my heart that my grandmother is now in God's presence, free from suffering, filled with joy, and held forever in His eternal love.

Her words still echo in me today: *"Something beautiful is coming."* They remind me that even in the darkest moments, God is at work, bringing beauty from sorrow, and preparing us for things greater than we can yet see.

Chapter 2

Childhood & Early Protection

Let me take you back to when I was just a baby—about 10 months old. My grandmother was babysitting me that day. We were in the kitchen, and I was in one of those walker things that help babies learn how to walk. Somehow, I managed to maneuver my way to the doorway and fell down a concrete stairway that led out to the backyard.

My grandmother was hysterical, beside herself with grief. As I've been told, I was in the hospital for quite some time. The doctors examined me over and over, running tests, taking scans, conferring in hushed voices outside my hospital room. My family gathered, waiting for news, fearing the worst.

The impact had caused my head to indent from the hit to the ground, but somehow—miraculously—it never touched or damaged my brain. The doctors had no medical explanation for it. By all accounts, with that kind of fall, there should have been severe brain damage. But there wasn't. Not even a trace. Because I was still so young, the doctors were able to work with my skull and get my head back to its proper shape.

Looking back on that moment now, I think of Psalm 121:3-4: *"He will not let your foot slip—he who watches over you will not slumber; indeed, he who watches over Israel will neither slumber nor sleep."* While I slept in that hospital bed as an infant, completely unaware of the danger I had just survived, God was awake. He was watching. His eyes never closed. My grandmother understood this in a way that transcended medical science. She knew that what she had witnessed wasn't luck or chance. It was divine intervention. God had caught me when I fell.

As I got older, my grandmother would tell me about that day. Her voice would grow soft but serious, and she'd look at me with eyes that seemed to see something I couldn't yet understand. She wouldn't just tell me the story casually, like recounting an old memory. No, she would sit me down, take my hands in hers, and speak with the weight of someone delivering a prophetic word. "You are special to God," she would say. "He has His mighty angels protecting you."

She explained something that seemed almost frightening at the time: when the devil tries to hurt you at such a young age, it's because you have a special calling. She told me that the enemy doesn't waste his time attacking ordinary lives—he goes after those whom God has marked for purpose. And that fall, that near-tragedy, was the enemy's first attempt to stop what God had already set in motion. You can imagine how a young girl might receive those words—I felt so special, like God's favorite! I walked around with this secret knowledge tucked in my heart, not fully grasping the weight of what she meant. I didn't really know how serious that really was.

My grandmother wasn't just speaking from emotion or grandmotherly affection. She was speaking from a place of spiritual discernment. She had lived long enough to recognize the spiritual warfare that most people miss. She had seen it in her own life, in her prayers, in the battles she fought on her knees. And now she was seeing it play out in mine. Jeremiah 1:5 tells us, *"Before I formed you in the womb I knew you, before you were born I set you apart."* God had set me apart before I took my first breath, and the enemy recognized it even when I was too young to understand it myself.

My grandmother told me there would be more challenging times in my life because of who I am and the gifts God has given me. At the time, I couldn't comprehend what she meant. I was just a little girl who wanted to play with dolls and help in the kitchen. I didn't understand calling or spiritual warfare or divine purpose. But she was planting seeds that would one day make sense. Seeds that would sustain me when I needed them most. But now, as an adult who has walked through valleys I never imagined, I understand. She knew. Somehow, she knew.

Psalm 91:11-12 became the anchor of her prophecy over my life: *"For he will command his angels concerning you to guard you in all your ways; they will lift you up in their hands, so that you will not strike your foot against a stone."*

This wasn't just a comforting verse to her—it was a reality she had witnessed. She had seen me fall down those concrete stairs. She had seen my head indent. She had watched the doctors shake their heads in amazement that there was no brain damage. And she understood what I was too young to grasp: this was supernatural protection.

Psalm 34:7 says, *"The angel of the Lord encamps around those who fear him, and he delivers them."* My grandmother feared the Lord, and her prayers created an encampment of angelic protection around me. I imagine now, looking back, that there must have been angels at the bottom of those stairs, cushioning my fall, redirecting the impact, guarding my fragile infant brain from the trauma it should have sustained. I picture them standing watch over my hospital bed, invisible to the doctors but visible to my praying grandmother. I believe with all my heart that my grandparents' prayers have protected me—still, even today. Their intercession created a hedge around me that I'm only now beginning to fully appreciate.

The devil tried to take me out before my story even began. But because "I AM"—because God exists, because He sees, because He had a plan for my life—I'm protected. I'm still here.

***

Growing up in my grandparents' house shaped everything about who I would become. That house on Madison Avenue became my entire world. Every room held a memory, every corner told a story. It was more than just a physical structure; it was a fortress of faith, a training ground for the battles I would later face. My parents had separated when my sister and I were young. My dad struggled with drinking, and my earliest memories of them together are filled with loud voices, yelling, and the sound of breaking glass. I wish things had been different. I wish my parents could have stayed together. But God had different plans.

Psalm 68:5-6 says, *"A father to the fatherless, a defender of widows, is God in his holy dwelling. God sets the lonely in families."* Even when my biological family was fractured, God set me in a family—with my grandparents—where I would be loved, protected, and taught the ways of the Lord. He didn't abandon me to chaos; He placed me exactly where I needed to be.

My mom was trying to find herself, navigating her own struggles. She was young, overwhelmed, and trying to piece together a life that had fallen apart. I don't think she knew how to be what we needed at that time, and that's okay. God knew. He had already made provision. In the midst of their brokenness, my grandparents stepped in and raised us—my sister and me. And we adored them. One thing that was certain although things were bumpy, my parents loved us with all they had!

I'm content with everything I have that God gave us the best life possible with our grandparents. He didn't give us a cookie-cutter family, but He gave us something better. He was molding us, shaping us, preparing us. Isaiah 64:8 reminds us, *"Yet you, Lord, are our Father. We are the clay, you are the potter; we are all the work of your hand."* God was the potter, and my grandparents' home was the wheel upon which He shaped me.

Looking back now, I don't hold grudges against my parents. I see them as people who were simply navigating through life, doing the best they could with what they had. Nobody is perfect. This life doesn't come with a manual. Romans 3:23 tells us, *"for all have sinned and fall short of the glory of God."* My parents were no exception, and neither am I.

Today, my mom is my ride or die. I go to her for everything. She's my best friend. It wasn't always like that growing up—relationships take time and nurturing and forgiveness. But I see all versions of my mom now as an adult, and I appreciate her for who she is. She is not me. She is not my grandma. She is herself—designed by God. Ephesians 2:10 says, *"For we are God's handiwork, created in Christ Jesus to do good works, which God prepared in advance for us to do."* My mother is God's handiwork, fearfully and wonderfully made, just as I am.

I can't imagine my life without her.

***

Our home at my grandparents' house was always full. "Normal" for us meant a busy household with laughter, chaos, and love spilling out of every room. My grandfather was the disciplinarian with a teddy bear heart. He always took care of me and my sister. He was the kind of man who commanded respect just by walking into a room, but the moment you needed him, his eyes would soften, and you knew you were safe. My grandmother—I called her Mommy because I was with her all the time. She was my world.

My uncles Edwin and Albert were always kids at heart. Spending time with them was full of fun and laughter. They always watched over us. My two other uncles, Ricky and Papo, were away in the Army and Marines, but when they came home, our house felt complete. I love them all so much.

When my uncle Albert eventually moved to Florida, I cried that night like my heart was breaking. I couldn't understand why he had to leave, why our family circle had to shrink. I remember pressing my face into my pillow, trying to muffle my sobs, feeling like a piece of our home had been torn away. My uncle Edwin was fighting his own demons, struggling with addiction and trying to navigate life, and it was really hard to watch someone I loved struggle so deeply.

This was our family life—not your typical sit-at-the-table-with-Mom-and-Dad kind of life. But I wouldn't have changed it for the world. I loved living there. I loved the people God chose to mold me.

Proverbs 22:6 instructs, *"Start children off on the way they should go, and even when they are old they will not turn from it."* My grandparents didn't just house me; they started me on the way I should go. Every prayer whispered over me, every scripture spoken in my presence, every example of faith lived out before my eyes—these were deposits into my spirit that would sustain me through storms I couldn't yet imagine.

My beautiful aunt used to come over every day, and we would all sit in the kitchen just talking, laughing, and drinking cafecito. Man, those were the best times! The smell of that Bustelo coffee would fill the entire house, rich and strong. My aunt would pull up a chair, my grandmother would pour, and the stories would start flowing. They'd talk about everything like family, faith, struggles, victories. I'd sit there absorbing every word, learning what it meant to do life together. My grandfather was always knocking something down to rebuild in the house. He was so handy, and I learned so much from him. I followed him around like a shadow, always watching him paint, lay tile, fix things. He never shooed me away or told me I was in the way. Instead, he'd hand me a tool, show me how to hold it, and teach me the proper technique. "Measure twice, cut once," he'd say. "Do it right the first time." Those lessons didn't simply revolve around carpentry. They were about life, about integrity, about taking pride in your work. Those moments taught me that you could create something beautiful with your hands if you were willing to work.

There was something sacred about those kitchen gatherings—the way my family circled around that table, the warmth of the coffee, the sound of laughter bouncing off the walls. Psalm 133:1 captures it perfectly: *"How good and pleasant it is when God's people live together in unity!"* That kitchen was a sanctuary, a place where unity wasn't just an idea but a daily practice.

But more than anything, my grandparents taught me about prayer. They taught me to love the Lord. They were the epitome of love and commitment—a living testimony of what faith looks like when it's woven into the fabric of daily life. What a blessing from God to have their example.

I would watch my grandmother pray, and it wasn't performative or showy. It was intimate, like she was talking to someone she knew deeply and trusted completely. She would close her eyes, and sometimes tears would stream down her face. Other times, she'd smile like she was listening to good news. She prayed over meals, over visitors, over situations, over dreams, over fears. She prayed in Spanish, in English. Prayer was as natural to her as breathing. 1 Thessalonians 5:17 tells us to *"pray continually,"* and she embodied that. Prayer wasn't an event for her; it was a conversation that never really ended.

Their lives became the foundation upon which my own faith would later be tested and refined. 2 Timothy 1:5 speaks of *"sincere faith, which first lived in your grandmother Lois and in your mother Eunice and, I am persuaded, now lives in you also."* Just as Timothy inherited faith from the generations before him, I inherited faith from my grandparents. Their prayers, their example, their unwavering trust in God—these became my inheritance, more valuable than any material possession they could have left me.

I didn't know it then, but everything they poured into me—the prayers, the faith, the love, the stories, the discipline, the laughter—was preparing me for the storms I would face. When I would later stand in hospital rooms over dying loved ones or when I would fight panic attacks that made me feel like I was losing my mind, it would be their voices I'd hear. Their prayers would rise up from the depths of my spirit like an anchor, keeping me from drifting away completely. God was building something in me through them, something that would hold firm when everything else felt like it was falling apart.

Deuteronomy 6:6-7 commands, *"These commandments that I give you today are to be on your hearts. Impress them on your children. Talk about them when you sit at home and when you walk along the road, when you lie down and when you get up."* My grandparents lived this scripture. They didn't just take me to church on Sundays; they brought God into our everyday life. He was present in the kitchen, in the backyard, in the laughter, in the discipline, in the quiet moments before bed.

The devil tried to take me out before I could even walk. But my grandparents stood in the gap. They prayed. They believed. They declared God's protection over my life.

Job 22:28 promises, *"What you decide on will be done, and light will shine on your ways."* My grandmother decided that I had a special calling. She spoke it over me. She declared angelic protection over my life. And God honored those declarations.

Years later, when I would face trials that seemed designed to destroy me, I would hear her voice in my spirit: "You are special to God. He has His angels protecting you." Those words would come back to me in emergency rooms and seasons when I felt completely alone. They would remind me that I was never fighting my battles by myself—that the same angels who caught me as an infant were still standing guard and responding to prayers that had been prayed years before. Those words became a lifeline that I wasn't facing these battles alone.

Proverbs 13:22 says, *"A good person leaves an inheritance for their children's children."* My grandparents left me an inheritance—not of money or property, but of faith, prayer, and the knowledge that I am covered by the hand of God. That inheritance has sustained me through losses, through grief, through medical trauma, through seasons of doubt. It is an inheritance that cannot be stolen, cannot depreciate, and will carry me all the way home to heaven.

And Because "I AM" heard their prayers, I'm still here to tell this story.

Because God is faithful to every generation, the seeds they planted in me and my mom continue to grow, even now.

Because my grandparents understood that their role was not just to raise me, but to introduce me to the One who would never leave me nor forsake me.

The concrete stairs that should have ended my story became the beginning of my testimony. The injury that could have destroyed my brain became evidence of divine protection. The childhood that could have been defined by brokenness became a foundation of faith.

Psalm 127:3 declares, *"Children are a heritage from the Lord, offspring a reward from him."* I was their heritage, their reward. And through their faithful stewardship of that gift, I learned who I truly belonged to—not to them, but to the God who formed me, who knew me, who set me apart, and who commands His angels to guard me in all my ways.

The enemy saw the calling on my life before I did. But my grandparents saw it too, and they made sure I would survive to walk it out.

Chapter 3

Teen Motherhood & Struggles

The pregnancy test sat on the bathroom counter, those two pink lines screaming louder than any words ever could. I was sixteen years old—barely one week past my sixteenth birthday—and the world as I knew it collapsed in an instant. My hands trembled so hard that I nearly dropped the test. I turned it over again and again, as if seeing it from a different angle could somehow change the result. The silence around me felt suffocating. I could hear my own heartbeat pounding like a drum against the walls of my chest, and for the first time in my young life, I truly felt what it meant to be afraid.

Only days earlier, I had been celebrating my sweet sixteen, surrounded by laughter, music, and the smell of birthday cake. I was still wrapped in the warmth of childhood—dreaming about my future, my music, and the life that stretched out before me like an open road. I never imagined that road would twist so suddenly, leading me to a place where innocence met responsibility in the most unforgiving way. The air felt heavy that morning as I stared at that test, my breath uneven. Somewhere deep inside, I heard a whisper I didn't yet understand: "Take courage. It is I. Don't be afraid." (Matthew 14:27). But courage felt like a foreign language that day.

My close friend had suspected something was wrong. I had been sick for days—nauseated, tired, unable to shake the exhaustion that clung to me like fog. She bought the test, pressed it into my hands, and stood outside the bathroom door in silence. When I opened the door, tears streaming down my cheeks, she didn't ask a single question. She just held me. Her arms became the only place I could breathe. "What am I going to do?" I kept whispering. Over and over. The question hung in the air, unanswered. She didn't have the words, and neither did I.

At sixteen, I was still a child myself—someone who should've been worried about exams, not diapers. I remember thinking how unfair it all felt. But even in my panic, somewhere beneath the noise of my fear, a quiet truth stirred. Psalm 139:13 says, "For You created my inmost being; You knit me together in my mother's womb." I didn't realize it then, but that verse wasn't only about the baby inside me. It was about me too. God had been knitting the threads of my life, even through the chaos, preparing me for a role I hadn't asked for but was destined to fill.

When I told my boyfriend, he looked as terrified as I felt. We were two scared kids holding onto each other in a storm we couldn't control. He wanted to be strong for me, but I could see the fear in his eyes. I think, in that moment, we both understood how quickly dreams could turn into duties. We were still figuring out who we were, and now we had to figure out how to be parents. The thought made my stomach twist.

That night, I couldn't sleep. I sat by my window, staring at the moonlight spilling across my room, whispering prayers I didn't even know how to form. "God, please help me. Please send someone who can understand." The next day, I got my answer when I heard my Uncle Edwin's keys jingling at the front door. I had been praying he'd come home sober enough to talk to. He'd battled his own demons, but he had the biggest heart of anyone I knew.

When I saw him, the words just spilled out. "I'm pregnant," I whispered, barely able to lift my head. He didn't yell. He didn't scold. He didn't tell me I'd ruined my life. He just pulled me into his arms. "Don't worry," he said softly. "We're going to figure this out." That moment taught me more about grace than any sermon ever could. Proverbs 17:17 says, "A friend loves at all times, and a brother is born for adversity." My uncle was proof of that truth.

He went to talk to my grandparents—my "Mom and Dad," the ones who had raised me. I stayed in my room, pacing and praying. At first, their voices were calm. Then the volume rose. And rose. Until it felt like thunder rolling through the walls. I sat on the edge of my bed, clutching a pillow against my chest, as their disappointment echoed through the house. My grandmother's voice broke my heart; she sounded like she'd aged ten years in a single conversation. My grandfather was calm, but my Mom's anger came from fear—fear that my life was about to fall apart before it even began.

When they called my father, the silence afterward was louder than the shouting. He walked all the way down Madison Avenue to the pharmacy where my boyfriend worked. Later, I heard the story of how my father reached across the counter, grabbed him by the shirt, and said with every ounce of fury and love he had: "You're going to marry my daughter." I wasn't there to see it, but I could imagine the scene perfectly—Just a Dad trying to protect his daughter.

That night, our house filled with family. My uncles, my aunt, my grandparents, my boyfriend, his sister—everyone crammed in the basement living room like a courtroom where I was both the accused and the defendant. I sat in the middle of it all, heart pounding, wondering if this was how my story would end. But something unexpected happened. Instead of judgment, I felt love. It wasn't quiet or easy, but it was real. My Uncle Ricky, calm and deliberate, spoke about responsibility and grace. My Aunt Titi Emily reminded everyone that I was still a child, that love didn't end when mistakes began. And Uncle Edwin, with his raspy voice and weary eyes, kept repeating, "We're going to get through this." He even joked and said "I'm going to be a great Uncle!" His love language is so evident in humor!

Romans 8:28 says, "And we know that in all things God works for the good of those who love Him." That night, I didn't fully believe it, but I felt it. Love was working in the chaos. It wasn't pretty or perfect, but it was present. For the first time since I'd seen those pink lines, I didn't feel alone.

The following months were a blur of change and growth. The gossip at school, the sideways glances, the shame—it all became part of my daily life. My mom transferred me out of regular high school to a special school for pregnant teens. I was so sad leaving behind what I was used to but going to the new school was best. I did so well there I even got to graduate a year early as I was put in the accelerated program. I left behind my grammar school friends, my teenage routines to welcome a new mindset of responsibility. Faith became a part of my daily life. I prayed constantly. Not fancy prayers, just honest ones. "Lord, give me strength. Help me not to fall apart." I began to understand what it meant to walk by faith and not by sight (2 Corinthians 5:7). Each day was an act of surrender.

When July 4th arrived, I found myself in a hospital room, holding a tiny miracle in my arms. I was in labor for over 18 hours. That day feels like yesterday. My daughter Nina was born—seven pounds, three ounces of pure grace. I remember looking at her tiny face and thinking, *How could God trust me with something so perfect?* She was my Independence Day in more ways than one. I had lost the freedom of childhood, but I'd gained a new kind of freedom—the freedom that comes from love.

As I rocked her in my arms, Philippians 4:7 came alive for me: "And the peace of God, which surpasses all understanding, will guard your hearts and minds in Christ Jesus." I didn't understand how peace could exist in such chaos, but it did. God's presence filled that hospital room, soft and steady, like light filtering through broken glass.

Motherhood changed me overnight. There was no time to ease into it. I was still in high school, working full-time, juggling diapers and deadlines. Some nights, I cried myself to sleep out of sheer exhaustion. But every morning, I woke up and kept going. I told myself I wouldn't be another statistic, another forgotten story of a teen mom who gave up. Galatians 6:9 became my lifeline: "Let us not grow weary in doing good, for at the proper time we will reap a harvest if we do not give up."

Every new opportunity felt like His hand guiding me. Isaiah 45:2 says, "I will go before you and make the crooked places straight." That's exactly what He did. Even when I felt unworthy, He kept making a way. I started to understand more and more of Joseph's Journey in Genesis 37:24 from the pit to the palace. From slavery to position.

Just when I began to find balance, life threw another storm my way. I found out I was pregnant again—this time at seventeen. I remember sitting on my bed, holding another test, my heart heavy with disbelief. My sister was the first to know. Her face turned pale; her eyes filled with hurt. She didn't yell, but her silence spoke volumes. Later, she told my mother, and the anger that followed felt like fire. I understood it. I truly did. My mother saw my future closing in on itself, saw me walking into a storm she couldn't shield me from.

But I couldn't end that pregnancy. The thought never crossed my mind. Jeremiah 1:5 echoed in my heart: "Before I formed you in the womb, I knew you." That verse was no longer abstract—it was alive. My son, Victor Jr., was not a mistake. He was chosen.

Still, the weight of it all pressed hard. I married my boyfriend to "make things right," but youth and fear don't build a foundation strong enough to weather real life. When he drifted away, lost in his own confusion and immaturity, I was left standing with two children and a determination that could only have come from God.

Those years were grueling. I worked full-time, went to school, and tried to build a home for my babies. We had a one-room apartment that smelled faintly of baby powder and hope. It wasn't much, but it was ours. There were nights I counted coins to buy milk. Days when the loneliness felt unbearable. And yet, in those moments, I'd look at my children and see light. Their smiles reminded me that even when I was sinking, Jesus was still reaching out His hand.

The story of Peter walking on water became my reflection in the mirror. When Peter saw the waves, he began to sink. Fear made him forget who was standing right in front of him. That was me—stepping out in faith, then drowning in fear, over and over again. But every time I cried out, "Lord, save me!" He caught me. Every unexpected blessing, every job offer, every moment of laughter from my kids was His hand keeping me above the surface.

Some nights, when the kids were asleep, I'd sit by the window and talk to God like a friend. "I'm trying, Lord," I'd whisper. "But I'm tired." And somehow, peace would come. Not always relief, not always answers, but peace. Psalm 46:1 says, "God is our refuge and strength, an ever-present help in trouble." That verse became my heartbeat.

I was far from perfect, but I was persistent. I kept showing up. I kept believing that somehow, God would redeem every tear, every struggle, every sleepless night. And He did. Slowly, quietly, in ways I couldn't always see.

Years later, when I looked back at that sixteen-year-old girl holding a pregnancy test, I didn't see failure anymore. I saw faith. I saw a girl who stepped out of the boat and dared to walk on water, even when the waves were wild. I saw a mother who learned that grace doesn't mean the absence of struggle—it means God's presence in the midst of it.

Every breath I took during those years was a testament to His mercy. Because of I AM, I survived. Because of I AM, I learned to walk again when I should have drowned. And though I stumbled many times, His hand never let go.

Chapter 4

Abuse, Divorce & Finding Worth

After having my first child on the 4th of July, I was changed forever! I knew God was with me! How could he give me a 16-year-old a baby? Did he think I could do this? I didn't know the first thing about being a mom. Someone's life is now in my hands! I had to grow up pretty fast! No time for figuring it out! Suck it up, buttercup was my mentality! I was fighting so hard not to be the statistic. I went to school full-time and worked full-time to pay for a small one-room apartment. But God always provided for me! He always put me on the path to gain life skills and amazing work environments!

In Exodus 4:10-12, Moses stood before the burning bush, protesting his inadequacy: *"I have never been eloquent... I am slow of speech and tongue."* Yet God's response cuts through every excuse we've ever made: *"Who gave human beings their mouths? Now go; I will help you speak and will teach you what to say."*

I mean, I was just trying to figure out life myself. But the same God who helped him part the sea was helping me part the chaos. The God who equips is the same yesterday, today, and forever. He doesn't call the qualified, He qualifies the called. And if that was true for Moses, then it was sure true for me. Because honestly, I didn't have a clue what I was doing. But somehow, He kept showing up, steady and faithful, teaching me as I went.

So, just when I thought I had my footing, life shifted beneath me again. It's funny how peace can feel like a pause instead of a promise when you've lived through enough chaos. It was 10 months later I got pregnant again with my second child. I confided in my sister. She was so upset with me that she let the cat out of the bag and told my Mom. I remember that day, I could hear canon balls in my head. I felt so hurt that she told on me but I could understand why everyone was so upset! Another kid and the Father totally absent and unreliable. I'm 17 now and my Mom didn't want me to go through with it. She was thinking about my future and how hard it was going to be for me with 2 kids. In my heart, I was so in love and blinded I couldn't see the storm I would soon be walking into.

You see, young love does that to you. It can make you blind as a bat. Seriously, experiencing it firsthand, it's like walking around in a fog so thick you could miss red flags the size of billboards. Hosea 4:6 warns, *"My people are destroyed for lack of knowledge."* But sometimes it's not that we don't know better, it's that we don't *want* to know better. We see what we want to see, and I was queen of that club. I had all the signs. Unfaithfulness, absence, unreliability. Yet I kept going back to that same dry well, thinking maybe this time the water would be fresh. Spoiler alert: it wasn't.

My husband, cause yeah, we got married to "do things right", ended up not being involved; he was young too and was in the era of playing the field. I was on my own working, going to school, and providing for these two humans who deserve a wonderful life, and by God, I was gonna bust my behind to give it to them! My daughter Nina and my son Victor Jr. were my life! We kinda grew up together, so to speak. They were teaching me how to be a mom, and I was teaching them at the same time. I might not have known all the right things mothers do, being so young, but all I knew was I was gonna give them the world.

The weight of single motherhood at seventeen, that kinda loneliness is a tad bit hard to explain. Like the burden of diapers and daycare and dollars stretched too thin wasn't enough, there was the soul-deep exhaustion of being everything to everyone on top of it. And all that while I myself felt like nothing to the one person who should have stayed. I quietly dealt with the absence of someone I truly loved, knowing he was not present in my life or our children's lives. But you know what? God had other and better plans. In 2 Corinthians 12:9-10, Paul discovered a counterintuitive truth: *"When I am weak, then I am strong."* And let me tell you, that was me all the way. My weakness became the canvas upon which God painted His strength. Every job I wasn't qualified for but somehow got, every bill that got paid when the math said it shouldn't, every time I didn't just fall apart, that was Him showing up for me.

And so, as a baby in Christ, I always taught them the value of believing in Jesus and the resurrection and to be good-hearted humans. My son Victor kept me on my toes... He was so full of energy. I knew God blessed me every time I looked into their eyes. I just wanted to be someone they would be proud of. I found that so hard to believe since I messed up and let myself get pregnant so young. With my "what a failure" mindset, I was so unkind to myself. I never gave myself grace. I worked hard to fight those voices in my head. But even then, there were times I felt the Lord provide a way out of my own insecurities. He ALWAYS provided!!

But you know, the enemy's biggest trick is not temptation, it's accusation. That voice in your head that says you're not enough, that you've messed up too much, that God's done with you? That is not God, that is the cursed one. Revelation 12:10 calls him *the accuser of our brothers and sisters, who accuses them before our God day and night."* In my case, too, he kept running his mouth nonstop, trying to make me believe I was disqualified. Whispering the same lie he's been telling since Eden: *You're not enough. You've ruined everything. God couldn't possibly use you now.* But as Romans 8:1 shuts that lie down with a single sentence: *"Therefore, there is now no condemnation for those who are in Christ Jesus."* I'd find relief in it. There isn't any condemnation for me. None. Not some. Not conditionally. None. Phew!

Somehow, God always gave me great jobs! Like seriously, I would get offered jobs in corporate settings with no experience, getting paid well, and getting all the benefits I needed for my kids! There is no convincing me that it was by chance, NO, God opened those doors! I could've easily fallen into deep depression and God kept me happy and focused on my kids and being a good Mom!

Because of, I AM!! Yes GOD!

Job 22:28 declares, *"You will also decree a thing, and it will be established for you; and light will shine on your ways."* I joke you not but I've seen this play out in my life more times than I can count. Every door that should've stayed shut, somehow swung open anyway. Every interview where someone looked past my paper-thin résumé saw something in me I couldn't even see in myself. Every paycheck somehow stretched further than it had any right to. These weren't coincidences or lucky breaks. It was my beloved God, who ceaselessly lined things up and made a way to show me He's been ahead of me the whole time.

***

It took a long time to get wise, because I kept falling back in *"Love"* with my kid's father. We'd break up, get back together and he was never faithful, and I knew it! My self-worth was so out the window! I actually believed him when he said I would never find anyone who would love me with 2 kids.

Meanwhile, Proverbs 26:11 offers an uncomfortable mirror: "As a dog returns to its vomit, so fools repeat their folly." Ouch. Harsh words, but true ones. I wasn't in love; I was hooked on the same pain that kept breaking me. I don't know how to explain this but there's a strange comfort in familiar hurt. At least you know what's coming and can brace for the fall. The unknown felt scarier than the same old heartbreak.

But then there's Hosea and that whole book is about a God who loves His unfaithful people anyway. Who keeps pursuing them, even when they keep running the other way. If He could love Israel through her mess, then maybe He could love me through mine, too, involving the kind of "adultery" where you keep choosing broken people over the One who never breaks you.

But I knew our journey together was ending because a part of me wanted more and I knew somehow God did not want me suffering anymore! Let him go! Let him go! I heard in my head so many times! In my heart, I knew I had to obey that voice, because God was protecting me from years of trauma!

That same still, small voice that told Elijah to step out to the mouth of the cave (1 Kings 19:12–13) — that's the voice I heard in the dark of my own bedroom: *"Let him go."* It wasn't loud enough to shake the walls. It just whispered. God doesn't compete with all the noise; He waits. He waits for the quiet, when you're too tired to fight back, when your walls start to fall, when your soul finally gets still enough to listen. That's when He speaks, soft, steady, unmistakable.

What I hadn't told anyone, not even myself for the longest time, was just how dark things had really gotten. There was verbal and physical abuse. He slammed me up against the wall one day in front of the kids. Nobody was around to save me. I was this little thing 90lbs. I didn't want the kids to start crying, and I just kept quiet and shrank in fear. I instantly had flashbacks of my mom and Dad when we were little. When my dad drank, it wasn't pretty. I think I only told my closest friend once because I didn't know what to do. I didn't want a future like this for my kids, so I finally walked away from my first love! Freedom for me felt like a good night's sleep!

Psalm 34:18 became more than words on a page that night, it became real. *"The Lord is close to the brokenhearted and saves those who are crushed in spirit."* God met me that night, not after I got it together, not after I healed, but right there in the wreckage. He didn't wait for me to be strong. He came into my weakness.

Just like in Judges 6:12, when the angel called Gideon a *"mighty warrior"* even while he was hiding, God saw more in me than I could see in myself. He saw the woman I was becoming, not the one I thought I'd ruined.

***

You know they say, hurt people, hurt people! I lived that!

He was hurt and broken in ways I could never fix as much as I wanted to. I always saw the good in him, even when he was kicking me down. I knew his heart wasn't completely lost and God could change that, too, but it wasn't my place. I had to understand I was NOT God, and he was not mine to fix!

The trap a lot of women fall into is mixing up compassion with responsibility. We see someone broken, and our hearts jump straight into rescue mode. I did that. I kept telling myself, *hurt people hurt people,* and it's true. But Ezekiel 18:20 makes it easy to get: *"The one who sins is the one who will die. The child will not share the guilt of the parent, nor will the parent share the guilt of the child."* His brokenness was real, but it wasn't mine to carry. His healing was needed, but it wasn't my job to make it happen.

The moment I tried to be his savior, I crossed a line I didn't even know existed. That's when compassion turned into control and when care became codependence. What I didn't realize was that I was stepping into God's lane, trying to do what only Christ can do. And trust me, that's a burden no heart can hold for long.

The harder part, though, was teaching my kids how to navigate this mess without carrying bitterness. Til this day, I have never been in a place of hating him, which I had so many reasons to fall into. I never shut the door on him being able to father his children. He just chose not to! It was later in life that he tried to grow those broken relationships with his kids. I taught my kids to forgive as Christ has forgiven us over and over so many times. It was hard for them to do that but they understood and finally slowly started letting him in. It wasn't without a battle. He was fighting his demons and never felt worthy enough or accepted. I could understand why he felt that way. His choices led him down that path.

Note how Colossians 3:13 doesn't leave much room for loopholes: *"Bear with each other and forgive one another if any of you has a grievance against someone. Forgive as the Lord forgave you."* It doesn't say *"forgive if they deserve it"* or *"forgive after they've changed"* or *"forgive when you feel like it."* Nope. It says *Forgive as the Lord forgave you.*

And how did He do that? Romans 5:8 spells it out: *"While we were still sinners, Christ died for us."* Before we got it together and said sorry.

Before we even cared. He forgave us while the nails were still in His hands. That's the kind of grace we're called to, not because it's easy, but because it's the only way to get free.

Forgiveness isn't approval. It's not pretending nothing happened, and it's definitely not letting someone back in to do it again. It's laying down your right to revenge and trusting God to balance the books. It's saying, *This debt is too heavy for me to carry. I'm putting it down.* And guess what? It's not for him, it's for me, for myself. Because carrying that weight only kept me tied to what God already wanted to release me from.

***

After a couple of years of being a single Mom, healing and learning who I was outside of that pain, God surprised me in the best way possible. I met someone who would change the dynamic of our lives. He was fun, full of humor and available to me in every sense of the word. Not what I was used to. I had to learn how to accept help, or how to realize it wasn't just me anymore. God really stepped it up this time! We got married on May 8, 2004. We met in 1997 but got married later. This man accepts me for me, loves me, loves my craziness, loves my imperfections, and is willing to love my kids as his own! I was always so concerned with who I would let around my kids! I felt truly blessed!

Quite like the rain that feels like a miracle after a drought. Or like a candle that looks like the sun after darkness. Isaiah 43:18–19 says it perfectly: *"Forget the former things; do not dwell on the past. See, I am doing a new thing! Now it springs up; do you not perceive it?"* And that's exactly what He did for me. God wasn't just giving me a new relationship; He was showing me something deeper. That I was worth being chosen. Worth being pursued. Worth a love that didn't come with bruises or conditions. A love that didn't require me to shrink just to fit inside someone else's brokenness.

Don't get me wrong, it wasn't always peaches and cream; we had work to do in our relationship, in working out our past relationship traumas that we carried into this new ship. It takes years to learn new ways and compromise. We loved each other but somehow we both needed to grow up in ways we couldn't teach each other. But God!

It felt as if the most honest two words in all of Scripture might just be in Mark 9:24: *"I do believe; help me overcome my unbelief."* The tug-of-war that I live in, and perhaps we all do: the "both/and" of faith. I loved him *and* I was scared. I trusted God *and* I carried wounds. I wanted this to work *and* I didn't know if I could do marriage without fear.

See, growth doesn't show up when life's easy. It happens right in the thick of the mess. 1 Peter 1:6-7 says our faith gets refined by fire, it's tested so its worth can shine through. And maybe that's what all of this was, God letting the fire burn off what wasn't faith, so what remained could finally be real.

There came a point where Gus and I hit a rough patch that tested everything we thought we'd built. It felt like all the progress was starting to crack under the pressure. I had separated from my husband. We just weren't getting along and needed time away from each other. Around that time, my aunt Laurie handed me a little piece of paper in church. She wrote this scripture verse on it. I didn't realize then how much I'd need those words, but God has a way of sending reminders right when your world starts to wobble.

That scripture was Proverbs 3:5-6, which said, *Trust in the Lord with all your heart and lean not on your own understanding, in all your ways acknowledge him, and he will make your paths straight.*

It was then that it occurred to me that at times, God's Word doesn't come through a burning bush or a thunderous voice from heaven; it comes in the form of a folded piece of paper slipped into your hand by someone who loves you. The Israelites kept Scripture on their doorposts and even on their foreheads (Deuteronomy 6:8–9). I kept mine in my pocket, edges worn soft from being touched a hundred times a day. It was a little lifeline when my mind forgot what my heart needed to remember: *Trust. Don't lean. Acknowledge. He will make straight.*

That word *"straight"* in Hebrew is *Yashar*, and it doesn't just mean straight. It means *right, pleasing, upright.* It dawned on me that God wasn't promising me an easy road but the right one. A path that might twist through valleys I didn't understand, but one that would still lead me exactly where He wanted me to be.

***

Through all these seasons of the abuse, the leaving, the healing, the new love, the struggles, one scripture kept showing up in my life like a refrain I couldn't escape.

For I know the plans He has for you, declares the Lord.

Jeremiah 29:11 played on in my own life for real, like it was the word alive through my journey! This was how God was helping me memorize scripture! By experiences I was living out.

Jeremiah spoke those words to people who were stuck and exiled in Babylon, wondering if God had packed up and left them for good. The full verse says, *"For I know the plans I have for you, declares the Lord, plans to prosper you and not to harm you, plans to give you hope and a future."* But what most of us skip over is the verse 10 right before it. *When seventy years are completed..."* Seventy years. Not seventy days. Not seven months. SEVENTY YEARS of waiting.

So you can't, by any chance, be mistaken there! Jeremiah wasn't promising a quick rescue. He was promising a slow redemption. The exile was real. The pain was real. But it wasn't permanent. Hebrews 11:13 says the heroes of faith *"died in faith, not having received the things promised, but having seen them and welcomed them from a distance."*

Sometimes God's promises stretch farther than our patience. Sometimes what He calls *prosperity* isn't comfort but *character*. The kind that can only grow when you learn to trust Him, even when the waiting feels like forever.

Looking back now with years of perspective, I can see what I couldn't see then. Marriage requires work; friendships require work. They are not always perfect. When I was dating my first boyfriend, my children's father, I went through so much. I was so blinded by love and being so young didn't help. I let myself become a doormat. It took a long while, but God taught me that I was valuable and worthy. There were times of verbal and physical abuse. So many times, my heart was broken over and over! You would think I'd hate him? but I didn't. I remember a conversation we had when we were young; He shared with me his fears and his struggles as a man. I actually felt sorry for him, not in a pitiful way, but kind of like I wanted to help him, but I grew to learn that wasn't my place.

Only God could help him.

In John 4, Jesus met a Samaritan woman at the well. This woman had five husbands and was now living with a man who wasn't her husband. Five attempts at finding worth in someone else. Five heartbreaks. And still, she tried again. But Jesus didn't shame her. He didn't list her mistakes. He offered her living water, which is a kind of love that doesn't run dry, doesn't abandon, doesn't leave you emptier than before.

My worth wasn't in whether I could fix him, nor was it in whether he stayed, or even in whether I was the perfect mom. Psalm 139:13–14 settles that once and for all: *"For you created my inmost being; you knit me together in my mother's womb. I praise you because I am fearfully and wonderfully made."* Past tense. Already done. Before I ever made a choice, good or bad. Before the success and the failure. Before the love and the loss. I was already valuable because the God of the universe said so.

***

The simple, powerful truth became the anchor of everything in my life. And that's what this is all about. Not the abuse, though that pain was real. Not the divorce, though that freedom was necessary. Not even the new love, though that healing was sweet. It's the realization that my worth was never up for negotiation. It was decided before time began, declared over me before my first breath, and secured on a cross two thousand years ago.

Because *I AM*, the great *I AM*, said I was worth dying for.

And if I'm worth *that*, then I'm worth fighting for. Worth protecting. Worth choosing myself when someone else won't choose me. Worth walking away from what's killing me, so I can walk toward what gives life.

Ephesians 2:10 says, *"For we are God's handiwork, created in Christ Jesus to do good works, which God prepared in advance for us to do."* The word *"handiwork"* in Greek is *poiēma*, where we get our word *poem*. You are God's poetry, not His rough draft or His mistake. You are His masterpiece.

The abuse tried to edit that poem. The lies tried to rewrite it. The shame tried to tear it up. But the Author doesn't allow unauthorized revisions. And because *I AM*, the poem continued past the violence, the fear, the broken marriage and into a new chapter. A chapter where worth isn't earned but received. Where love isn't taken but given and where the plans God had for me, plans to prosper and not to harm, were slowly, painfully, yet beautifully coming into focus.

Chapter 5

Divine Assignments - Listening to God's Voice

For a while after Gus and I got married, life felt like it was finally settling. We had our struggles, working through past traumas, learning to trust again. We were building something real. And then, like a storm you don't see coming, we hit a wall. We separated. We needed space. We needed time. And that's when God's voice broke through the noise again.

I remember waking up one day with a strong feeling that I had to move. My spirit was nudging me, *I need you to move, just listen to my voice!*

You ever have one of those moments where something hits you so hard you can't shake it? Like a knowing deep in your bones that won't let you rest? That's what this felt like. Not a gentle suggestion, but a holy shove. And here's the thing about God's voice—it doesn't always make sense to your brain, but your spirit recognizes it instantly. It's like when Samuel heard God calling him in the night (1 Samuel 3:10), and he kept thinking it was Eli. Sometimes we mistake God's voice for our own thoughts, or worry, or someone else's opinion. But when you finally recognize it, there's no mistaking it.

We were living in Florida at the time, and I wanted to move back up North to New Jersey. I prayed about it, and I asked God like is this what you want me to do Lord? It doesn't make sense; I have a good job here and a really nice townhouse apt. But something in my spirit was like tugging me like I had to go on this mission. I couldn't really explain it.

On paper, it was ridiculous. I had stability, comfort, a good situation. Why would anyone walk away from that? But Abraham didn't know where he was going either when God told him to leave his country (Genesis 12:1). He just packed up and went. That's the thing about divine assignments, they rarely come with a detailed roadmap and a risk assessment report. They come with a whisper and an invitation to trust.

I shared this thought with a friend in NY, and she mentioned to me, "I have a friend who works at a firm in NY and is hiring." What are the chances of that? So I sent in my resume and eventually, they scheduled a first interview via Zoom.

They wanted a second interview, but in person, so I flew up to NY, and boy, did I pray about this. I did this all afraid! A part of me felt like I didn't know what the heck was happening, like what was I doing? But then this strong feeling in my chest was like just listen to my voice!

See, obedience doesn't require the absence of fear. It requires movement in spite of it. Moses was afraid. Gideon was terrified. Esther risked her life. But they all moved when God said move. Courage isn't feeling brave; it's doing what you're called to do while your knees are shaking.

In the interview, I met with one of the owners of the firm and the HR Director. It was instantly, when I met the Partner of the firm, an older fellow in his late 70s, that I heard a voice say, "This is him". Would you believe me if I told you that something told me it was him I had to go there for? Like my God given mission was about him or for him. Hope that makes sense.

I did the interview, which was not easy. He was so sharp and knew all about taxes and questioned me on almost everything tax prep-related. He wanted to make sure everything that was on my resume was in my head! They were on the 22nd floor, and by the time I made it down the elevator to the first floor, I got the call that they were offering me the position and even gave me $10,000 more than what I asked for.

You could imagine my surprise, and also I was like Oh boy, this means I gotta go back to Florida and pack and resign and yada yada all the things!

When God opens a door, He doesn't crack it open a little bit; He flings it wide. The favor was undeniable. The timing was perfect. And the extra money? That was God saying, "I've got you. I know what you need before you even ask." Matthew 6:8 reminds us of this truth. Our Father knows what we need. And when He sends us on assignment, He equips us for it, financially, emotionally, and spiritually. Every single piece.

I went back to Florida to pack, got the kids' school paperwork, and in the meantime, I was trying to find an apartment in Jersey. I looked online, and I was like, I need to be there to see this place. No way was I getting an apartment without seeing it. But I found something online. It said New, with a washer and dryer, it looked like a Florida-style apartment. Meaning all the bells and whistles at a good price near the train station.

My sister, who lived in Jersey, went to look at it for me just to make sure. And even she couldn't believe it, she was like Wow, it's all brand new and beautiful. And if you don't know this, it's really hard to find an apartment in the metro area that has "new everything," let alone a washer and dryer. I took it and I just knew that it was all a blessing from God!! I knew it! My heart knew it, my spirit knew it and it filled me with this adrenaline joy unexplainable!

God was confirming every single step. The apartment shouldn't have been that perfect, that available, that affordable. But when you're walking in obedience, suddenly things that should be impossible become possible. Doors that should be locked swing open. Provision shows up exactly when you need it. This is what it looks like when Jehovah Jireh, the God who provides, goes ahead of you and makes a way.

Everything was working out! My family thought I was crazy for just getting up and leaving like this. But I didn't care! I knew God was sending me! There was nothing anyone could say or do to convince me otherwise!

And that's where the rubber meets the road, isn't it? When everyone around you thinks you've lost your mind, but you know you've found your assignment. When logic says stay, but God says go. When comfort whispers "don't risk it," but faith shouts "trust Me." This is the crossroads where true obedience is tested. Will you follow the crowd or follow the call?

We moved up north, and I started my new job, and boy, was that a humbling experience to say the least.

I had to take 3 trains and the subway to get to 5th Avenue, NY. In Florida, my commute was only 15 minutes. I traded that for almost an hour and a half, morning and evening commute.

Nobody tells you that obedience sometimes comes with discomfort. Following God doesn't always mean ease and convenience. Sometimes it means longer commutes, harder adjustments, steeper learning curves. But here's what I was learning: comfort isn't the goal. Character is. Growth is becoming who God created you to be. And sometimes that requires leaving behind what's easy for what's necessary. Anyway, when I started my job, I made a friend whose name was Hope!

She was such a sweet darling of a human! She introduced me to everyone and showed me the ropes. So, I was getting to know my new Boss, and he kinda reminded me of my Grandfather! His presence demanded reverence and respect! In my head, I was like, you better not mess up! As I got to know him, and he got to know me, I felt so honored to work for him!

He was thorough, honest, and wise! He did tax prep the old way, but in terms of modern-day tax prep. When I was around him, I sat up straight and kinda kept quiet, but then one night I realized God sent me to him, so I had to be myself and find out what he might need prayer for. Isn't it just like God to name my first friend there "Hope"? Because that's exactly what I needed in those early days. I needed hope that I hadn't made a terrible mistake, hope that this assignment made sense, hope that God knew what He was doing. And my boss, this dignified man who carried himself with such authority and wisdom, he reminded me of my grandfather for a reason.

God was showing me that He speaks our love language. He knows what makes us feel safe, what brings us comfort, and what helps us trust. He was putting the familiar in the midst of the foreign, anchoring me while everything else felt uncertain.

As the days went by, he would tell me all about his clients one by one, who was rich, who was sick, who had how many divorces, etc. What I found admirable was that he didn't judge any of them; he genuinely helped them, and I saw that in real time! I could see the years of experience and patience in his eyes! I respected him not just as a Boss but as a person. When I would go home at the end of the day, I would pray for his clients. Some of them had serious health issues.

As days went by, I got to learn about him and his wife and kids, whom he loved so much. I could tell in his smile when he mentioned them. His wife and I had something in common: we both loved singing. I would also pray for him every day! Also, one thing I forgot to mention is that this office was predominantly Jewish.

The assignment was becoming clearer. I wasn't just there to file taxes or answer phones. I was there to pray. To intercede. To stand in the gap for people who didn't even know they needed it. Ezekiel 22:30 talks about God looking for someone to stand in the gap. That's what intercessory prayer is, standing between heaven and earth, between God's will and someone's need, and praying until breakthrough comes. These clients may seem like mere names on files. But they were souls God loved, people with stories and struggles, and I got to be their secret prayer warrior. I would spend hours in the file room praying over names I've never seen.

Anyway, moving along, I got to know the rest of the office and made friendships. Some people were really going through hard things in life, and every day, I found myself praying for this group of people! I knew God sent me there for a reason! Things got better, and my Boss started bringing me a pear every day to work. I was so happy I felt like I was doing a good job, and he likes me I guess!

A pear every day. Such a small thing, but it meant the world. It meant I was seen, valued, accepted. Sometimes God's love shows up in a piece of fruit offered by someone who doesn't even realize they're being used by God. That's how sneaky-good He is. He'll use anyone and anything to remind you that you're exactly where you're supposed to be.

My time there was about 5 months. It was time for me to go. I ended up deciding to move back to Florida with no job, just wanted to be back. On the last day with the NY firm, they bought me a cake and food, and everyone came to say bye at the kitchen of the office. I remember asking my Boss if he would join me in the kitchen with the rest of the people to have lunch. He said yes.

When we walked in, some of the people were surprised by his attendance. One Lady said, "He never eats with the rest of the office. This was his very first time in years." When they asked him why he joined, he simply said, "Well, I was asked and invited, so I came."

Can you believe that? All it took was a simple invitation to the kitchen. Maybe that's what my purpose was. No, just kidding, I think it was far more than that!

Five months. That's all it took to complete the assignment. Short-term missions are no less significant than long-term ones. Sometimes God sends you somewhere just for a season, just for one person, just for one moment. And sometimes the smallest act, like inviting someone to lunch, can mean everything. That man hadn't eaten with his staff in years. But because someone asked, he came. Because someone included him, he participated. Never underestimate the power of an invitation, of reaching out, of making someone feel like they belong.

So, everyone returned to work, and as the day ended, I went into his office and asked him if I could speak to him in private. He said, "Of course," and I closed the door behind me. The whole day, God was telling me to tell him why I was there. I was so nervous that my armpits were wet from nervousness. Sorry for the TMI, but true story. *Like God! Why are you making me tell this man this truth. He is going to think I'm nuts!*

But if I didn't do this, I would regret it, and I didn't want to upset God! As if that would upset him, but my head was telling me this like a nutso!

This is how every divine assignment builds toward the moment where you have to open your mouth and say the thing God told you to say, even when it sounds crazy. Even when you're sweating through your shirt. Even when you're convinced the person will think you've lost your mind. But the truth is, God's assignments always require risk. They require vulnerability. They require you to look foolish for the sake of obedience. And sometimes, the very thing that feels most terrifying is the exact thing someone needs to hear.

I was in his office, and he sat down in front of me, and I began to tell him that God had sent me to NY for someone. I left Florida and didn't even know why; I just knew I had to obey. I told him the first day I met him, I felt the Holy Spirit tell me to pray for you. Then I asked him, "Would you allow me to pray for you right now"? He said, "Yes, of course," with no hesitation!

We held hands and closed our eyes, and I prayed for him. Then, when we opened our eyes, he was teary-eyed and said, "Maribel, you deserve to be happy!" May God bless your heart and your obedience!

And there it was. The reason for everything. The move, the job, the long commutes, the months away from home, it was all for this one prayer. This one moment of connection. This one opportunity to let someone know that God saw him, that God cared about him, that God had sent someone all the way from Florida just to pray for him. That's the extravagant love of God right there. He'll move mountains, orchestrate circumstances, and send His people across state lines just to reach one heart.

I felt so relieved at that very moment! Like I could breathe! *Like God, I did it! You did it!!* This man didn't reject me and embraced a prayer from a simple Jesus-fearing girl from Florida, whom he had only known for a few months.

It was time to say goodbye and he hugged me! I would never forget him, Mr. S. Glassman, a child of God.

Every year on his birthday till he passed away in early 2024, I always sent him a birthday message via email! I could never forget his birthday as it was the same as my Grandmothers! Another Godwink from the Lord! God doesn't forget the details. Even the birthday connection, same as my grandmother's, was God saying, "I'm weaving this story together in ways you won't understand for years, but trust Me, it's all connected." And the fact that I kept in touch with him, that I remembered him year after year until he passed, was much more than plain kindness. That was a covenant. That was honoring the assignment even after it officially ended. That was stewarding the relationship God had entrusted to me.

Because "I AM"..... that is what I heard in my spirit!

The greatest experience of faith in my life was doing something I couldn't understand, with opposition from everyone around me and seeing the fruits of the spirit!!

When I think of it, I'm filled with emotions of how Good God is!

This is what it means for Scripture to become living and active (Hebrews 4:12). Not just words on a page, but truth you walk through, breathe in, live out. While I may think God was teaching me verses, He was basically writing them into my story. Every step of obedience was a verse coming to life. Every answered prayer was Scripture proving itself true. Every divine appointment was God showing me that His Word doesn't just describe reality, it creates it.

One part I haven't talked about is all the other things I experienced in NY while I was there. Every day on the train or subway, I would run into prayer opportunities! I saw so many things that broke my heart. A mother with her newborn, sitting outside on the platform, begging for food. A Lady on the subway, yelling out, "There is no God," we are slaves! She was standing right next to me and on the subway, people were literally like sardines in a can!

Every day before getting home, I would pray so much! My body and mind would feel so drained. The energies I felt, I felt deep in my soul! It's hard to explain in words. Sometimes I would feel sick from all the pain I saw all around me. Like I could feel brokenness, pain, self-righteousness, greed, evil, etc. It was like walking into a sea of demonic forces. I had to constantly pray the shield of faith around me! Another scripture that God was bringing to life around me was: Ephesians 6:10-12 10 *"Finally, be strong in the Lord and in his mighty power. Put on the full armor of God, so that you can take your stand against the devil's schemes."* For our struggle is not against flesh and blood, but against the rulers, against the authorities, against the powers of this dark world and against the spiritual forces of evil in the heavenly realms.

Never think that Divine assignments are only about the one person you're sent to; they are about the territory you walk through to get there. Every train ride was a prayer journey. Every subway platform was a battlefield. I was learning what it meant to "pray without ceasing" (1 Thessalonians 5:17), to carry the presence of God into dark places, to stand firm when spiritual warfare was swirling all around me. This wasn't a glamorous ministry. This was trench warfare. This was showing up every single day in enemy territory and declaring that God's name is higher, His power is greater, His love is stronger.

Even though this season doesn't sound so great, it was!! I felt so joyful knowing God was in it! I didn't always like my job, and the commute was a pain, but that was the flesh screaming out of me! *Because I AM, Hallelujah, thank you Jesus!*

Joy isn't circumstantial. It's positional. It comes from knowing you're in the center of God's will, even when that center is a crowded subway car or a long commute or a difficult assignment. Paul and Silas sang in prison (Acts 16:25). Not because prison was fun, but because God was with them. That's the kind of joy I'm talking about, which doesn't make sense to anyone watching, but makes *perfect* sense to the one living it.

I return back to Florida and my husband and I reconcile. We bought a house with a pool in a beautiful neighborhood, and God blessed me with more than I could have ever imagined or felt worthy enough to receive! I was living my best life at this point!

As there is a blessing after obedience. Because here's what I was learning: when you say yes to God's assignments, even the hard ones, even the ones that don't make sense, He blesses you on the other side. Not always immediately. Not always in the way you expect. But always in ways that exceed what you could have imagined. The reconciliation, the house, the pool, the beautiful neighborhood, these weren't just nice things. They were God's "well done" for walking out the assignment He gave me.

***

Then came the day, my daughter called me to share the most amazing news that changed my life in the best possible way forever! "You're going to be a grandma." My heart literally burst with joy! I was so excited; all I could think of was how I was going to spoil this baby and be all the wonderful things my grandparents were for me! My love bug Avian aka Puti was born on March 12. His first Christmas, I didn't care how little itty bitty he was, I bought him a Power Wheels train set that took up the entire living room! I was so full of joy, I just wanted to pour into him every minute of every day. Every good and perfect gift comes from above, James 1:17.

Life was amazing, and I was living for this season where our family was growing! A year and a half later, another grandson was born, Anthony aka Chupi. These two were so different from each other, and I'm just thankful to God for the gift of their life! My heart is overjoyed. There's something about becoming a grandparent that feels like a second chance at joy. Like God giving you another opportunity to pour out love, to create memories, to leave a legacy.

I wanted to be for them what my grandparents were for me—a safe place, a source of unconditional love, a living example of faith. And for a while, everything felt like a dream. Two grandsons, healthy and perfect. A family growing and thriving. God's goodness on full display.

Fast forward to November 2018. Life had settled into this beautiful rhythm. The grandsons were thriving, Gus and I were solid, work was good. I was finally in a season where I could exhale. Where I wasn't waiting for the other shoe to drop.

My faith felt solid as a rock! Unshakable! I was sharing the good news of God with anyone who would listen and just trying to be a good steward. But as I learned, and would learn again, God doesn't keep us comfortable. He grows us and develops us. And sometimes, just when you think you've arrived at a place of unwavering trust, He asks you to trust Him deeper in ways you never imagined and with stakes you never wanted to face.

Then, one morning, I woke up with that feeling. You know the one, the holy nudge that won't let you rest. Avian had a slight cold, but nothing crazy. But I remember waking up and having this urge to tell my daughter to take him to the doctor. Now. She took him for a checkup, and they said he seems okay but his blood pressure was slightly elevated. The doctor said just to be on the safe side, take him in for a scan to check his heart. The next day, my daughter had to go back in for results, and I remember my husband went with her. I had a meeting at work, and I couldn't leave.

Later that afternoon, she called me at work, and I could hear in her voice that something wasn't right. She tells me, Ma, there is something wrong with his heart. The floor fell out from under my feet. My body felt numb with fear of the unknown. I had to keep it together for her. So, they told us he would need open heart surgery in the next month or so. He was only 3 years old. As you can imagine, this was risky and no sugar coating the facts. I asked everyone I knew to pray. I even posted on prayer sites, please pray for my grandson.

When the unthinkable happens, when the worst news comes, when the storm you never saw coming crashes into your life…that's when you find out if your faith is real. It's easy to trust God when the bills are paid and the kids are healthy and the sun is shining. But when the doctor says "open heart surgery" and the patient is three years old and he's your grandson, that's when faith either crumbles or crystallizes. That's when you either run toward God or run away from Him. And I'm telling you, there were moments I wanted to run. Moments I wanted to scream. Moments I wanted to demand answers.

I remember how strong my daughter was! She was like a pillar of strength and never once wavered from her faith! I was learning from her. Every day, I would go home and just break down in the shower. Powerless, I felt! How could I not fix this for my kid?

Sometimes your children teach you about faith. Sometimes the student becomes the teacher. I watched my daughter walk through this with a grace I didn't have. With a trust I was struggling to find. And it humbled me. Because I thought I was the one with the strong faith, the one who'd been through trials, the one who knew how to trust God. But here was my daughter, facing every parent's worst nightmare, and she wasn't falling apart. She was standing firm. And I was the one breaking down in the shower, the one feeling powerless, the one questioning everything.

My grandson had his surgery on Valentine's Day. The hardest part wasn't the surgery; it was the recovery afterwards. Watching him slowly come out of an open-heart surgery was the hardest thing I've ever had to live through. Watching my baby girl watch her baby go through this was unimaginable. I knew God was doing something, I just didn't understand at the time.

When times like this happen, you depend on your circle to help you through it. I had so many people praying and reaching out to see if we were all okay. We weren't, but we were trusting in God regardless. How much can my heart take? Life has been like a battlefield. A small voice I felt whisper I am with you. Isaiah 43:2 promises that when we walk through the fire, we won't be burned. Not that we won't walk through it. Not that we'll avoid it. But that, when we're in it, when the flames are all around us, when we can't see our way out—He's there. That small voice whispering "I am with you" was the same voice that whispered to Elijah in the cave, to David in the wilderness, to Paul in the prison. It's the voice that doesn't shout over the chaos but speaks into it, steady and sure.

Our family unit was tighter and just loving each other. I started to see the fruit even though it seemed unfair. My mentor, Maria, would call me to just offer advice on how to cope or to be mindful of taking care of myself. My Mom brain just wanted to fix things like I was always used to doing. I'm not God! I had to surrender it to the Lord! He delivered my grandson and healed him, and all things were starting to get back to normal. But the wounds were still fresh for all of us.

I've never been so proud of my daughter as I was when I saw her overcome. I've never been so proud of my other children for being there for her and supporting each other like they did. Love is a fruit that is always in season! My sorrow turned into singing! My tears turned into laughter at the sound of my grandson getting back to his normal self. God is so good! Storms are not meant to break us; they are meant to refine us!

And that's the lesson that took me a lifetime to learn. Storms aren't punishment. They're preparation. They're not meant to destroy you but to develop you. Romans 5:3-4 talks about how suffering produces perseverance, perseverance produces character, and character produces hope. That's the refining process. That's the fire that burns off the impurities and leaves behind something stronger, purer, more beautiful than what was there before. My grandson's healing wasn't just physical; it was also spiritual. It refined our family. It refined my faith. It showed me that God doesn't waste our pain; rather, He redeems it, transforms it, and uses it to make us more like Jesus.

The divine assignment to New York taught me to listen for God's voice and obey even when it made no sense. But my grandson's heart surgery taught me that obedience doesn't protect us from pain. Sometimes God sends us into assignments, and sometimes He sends us into storms. And in both, His voice remains the same: *"I am with you."* That's the truth that carried me through New York's subway platforms and Florida's hospital waiting rooms. Because I AM, the great I AM, doesn't just call us to assignments. He walks with us through the refining fire.

***

In another scenario, I was pregnant with my 4th child, and this pregnancy was considered high risk as I was carrying low. On the day I went into labor, I remember going into the hospital in unbearable pain. They checked me and said, "Three centimeters, hun" with a dismissive tone. The machine that reads contractions wasn't registering anything significant. "You have a ways to go," they told me, looking at me like I was one of *those* women, the ones who just want to have the baby already.

They left my husband and me in the room, waiting for Mother Nature to take its course.

An hour went by, and I told my husband that something didn't feel right. The pressure was overwhelming. "Babe, please check me, I feel something weird!" I yelled. Mind you, this wasn't my first rodeo. I'd had three other children. I knew what a contraction felt like, and this was different.

He lifted the blanket and screamed, "OMG, THE HEAD IS OUT!"

I was in excruciating pain, feeling completely helpless. No epidural, no medication, no preparation, just raw, unfiltered agony. I started yelling out, "Jesus! Jesus!" because in that moment, He was the only one who could help me.

My husband ran out for help and found a candy striper, a hospital volunteer, who rushed in and literally caught the baby. My husband even took a picture as proof of what was happening because he knew no one would believe this.

Then, finally, the nurse who had dismissed me earlier came rushing in, apologizing profusely. But I didn't want apologies. "Just check my baby," I said through tears.

They called my doctor, and when he arrived at the hospital, I could hear him in the hallway, his voice booming with righteous anger. "How could you depend on a machine to dictate if she was having contractions? Did you not read her chart? High risk! Three previous children! How could you leave her like that?"

He came into my room apologizing as well, but all I cared about was whether my baby was okay. And she seemed fine or so we thought.

Psalm 139:13-16 took on new meaning for me that day: *"For you created my inmost being; you knit me together in my mother's womb... My frame was not hidden from you when I was made in the secret place."* God had been there in that delivery room. He had sent a candy striper at just the right moment. He had protected my baby girl even when the medical staff failed us.

We went home, relieved and grateful. But a few months down the line, I noticed something wasn't right. Angel had this little water bubble on her head, and her head tilted to the right. I took her to the doctor, and they ran some tests. "She's fine," they assured me. "Nothing to worry about."

But a week went by, and that little bubble kept getting bigger. My gut feeling wouldn't go away. A mother's intuition is a gift from God, and mine was screaming that something was wrong.

I went back, and this time they sent me to the hospital for a scan.

I sat in the hospital room with my baby, waiting for results and praying silently. Then I noticed something strange: security guards were stationed at the door of my room. My heart started racing, but I tried to stay calm, continuing to pray for good results.

A nurse came in, her face serious. "We need you to come with us," she said. "Leave the baby here."

I was by myself, my husband was at work, and I had come straight from the pediatrician's office. They escorted me to the security office, and that's when they dropped the bomb.

"You're being investigated for endangering your baby."

My stomach dropped. I felt the blood drain from my face. "Are you serious?" I whispered, my voice breaking.

They explained that the scan showed a hematoma fracture to the skull. They didn't ask questions. They didn't ask for my side of the story. I was immediately guilty until proven innocent.

I was in tears, beside myself, because I had no one there to defend me. *I would never hurt my kids. They are my life!* I was the one who had been taking her to doctors over and over again, trying to find answers, and nobody would listen.

Hours crawled by. They allowed me to stay with Angel while I waited for my husband to arrive; his job was an hour away. During that agonizing wait, they called the police. An investigator arrived and informed me they would need to conduct lie detector tests on me, my husband, my younger kids, and even our babysitter.

I was terrified. Tears streamed down my face. I felt utterly alone.

One of the caseworkers looked at me and said bluntly, "If you don't pray, you better start."

I understood why they had protocols for situations like this. There are parents who genuinely mistreat their children, and those children need protection. But me? I was being treated like a criminal when all I had done was advocate for my daughter's health.

The investigator assigned to our case turned out to be kind. She told me she had taken her own kids to the same pediatrician and had similar frustrations with their care. When I explained how many times I had brought Angel in and been dismissed, she understood.

We all took the lie detector tests, and of course, we all passed. When we started taking Angel to therapy for her head tilt, the specialists realized the injury likely came from her traumatic birth, the very birth where the hospital had failed to monitor me properly.

All those hours waiting in that hospital, I remember thinking about how Jesus must have felt during the day leading up to His crucifixion. He was innocent, yet accused. He was blameless, yet condemned. He carried a cross He didn't deserve.

I felt like I was carrying a huge cross that day, and no one could hear me screaming my innocence.

How could this be happening to me? I'm a good mom, and they're treating me like a criminal.

But then, in the midst of my anguish, God shifted my perspective. I turned my storm into intentional prayer, not just for myself, but for children who truly are mistreated, for parents who struggle, for systems that fail vulnerable families.

At that moment, I realized: *If this is happening to me, so I can be an intercessor for these situations, then so be it.*

How could I understand the feeling of unjust persecution without having lived it? Because "I AM". Because God was there, He opened a new level of understanding in me. He renewed my mind to see beyond my own pain.

I envisioned a battlefield. I saw myself suiting up in spiritual armor every day, just as Ephesians 6:11-17 instructs: *"Put on the full armor of God, so that you can take your stand against the devil's schemes."*

I envisioned the arrows of the enemy flying by me, and I saw my prayers being carried by angels straight to the throne of God.

I knew God was with us. He had saved me once again.

My daughter was well. I met amazing people on this journey, people who showed me kindness when I expected judgment. He took that mustard seed of faith and turned it into what I like to call a "Loud Uncle Edwin Hallelujah!"

For those who don't know, my Uncle Edwin is unapologetically loud in his praise. His "Hallelujah!" can wake the dead, and I love it! That's the kind of faith God was building in me through this trial.

***

So do you believe in angels? Do you believe that God can step in and help you see something you wouldn't be able to see on your own?

Let me tell you about another moment when I witnessed divine intervention so clearly that it left me breathless.

We were at a family barbecue at the pool. There were a lot of us, and we'd been having a wonderful time all day. As the afternoon wound down, it was time to pack up. My husband was gathering the cooler and getting the stroller ready for our baby daughter, Angel. My 13-year-old son, Victor, was still in the pool, and my eldest daughter was collecting her things.

My 5-year-old son, Kenny, had just gotten out of the water. I had dried him off and removed his swimmies, those inflatable arm floats that help kids stay afloat.

I turned around to get baby Angel settled in the stroller. My husband called out, "I'm going to get the car!"

Then, out of nowhere, something supernatural happened.

I stood up straight. My head turned sharply to the right, as if someone had physically moved it. My eyes locked onto a specific spot at the bottom of the pool.

My heart sank.

There was Kenny, my 5-year-old, at the bottom of the pool, without his swimmies, motionless.

I screamed at the top of my lungs, "VICTOR! GET KENNY! HE'S RIGHT BEHIND YOU!"

Victor dove down and pulled his little brother out. Everyone rushed over. Kenny was coughing, sputtering, puking up water. His lips were tinged blue. My heart was racing so fast I thought it would burst out of my chest.

They told me I passed out from the shock and panic, I don't even remember that part.

One more minute. That's all it would have taken.

God *literally* turned my head in that exact direction at that exact moment. I wasn't looking at the pool. I had my back turned. There was no natural reason for me to suddenly look that way.

But God directed my face to that precise spot in the pool where my son was drowning.

I 100% believe He saved my son that day. He was there. He intervened. He moved my head like a divine hand guiding my gaze to where it needed to be.

Psalm 91:11 promises, *"For he will command his angels concerning you to guard you in all your ways."* I believe angels were at work that day, protecting Kenny, alerting me, orchestrating a rescue that defied natural explanation.

For two weeks after that incident, I couldn't sleep. Every night, I'd get up and check on my kids, watching them breathe, making sure they were safe. Every morning, I'd wake up thanking God for another chance, thanking Him for protecting us.

The enemy has been trying to break me, distract me, take me out, but GOD!

Because "I AM" was with me, I'm still here. Because "I AM" was watching over my children, they're still here.

These experiences drove me to church more often. I was yearning for God's Word like a person dying of thirst yearns for water. I always believed in God. I was raised Catholic, went to church, respected the name of Jesus but this was a whole new level of hunger for Him…

I used to take my kids and my niece to a little church near our house. The people were lovely, and I learned so much as a new Christian truly discovering what a personal relationship with Jesus meant.

I remember the pastor talking about how when we are called and chosen, the journey is hard. No sugar-coating. He gave it to us straight: *"Even though I walk through the valley of the shadow of death, I will fear no evil, for you are with me"* (Psalm 23:4).

Darkness does not comprehend the light (John 1:5). I began to understand the years of storms, struggles, rejection, mistreatment, and attacks of the evil one in a new way.

God was always there protecting me!

Because "I AM" loved me, I was never alone on this journey. He was always teaching me, refining me, preparing me for the moment I would return home to heaven.

I owe all the praise and worship these lungs can render to the King of Kings, the Father, the Friend, the one true intimate partner of my spirit, I AM!

No matter what this flesh cries out for, my spirit is saved. By His wounds, I am healed!

Yahweh, Jesus!

Chapter 6

Noah's Story - Loss & Shaken Faith

June of 2016. I was 42 years old, and life had finally settled into a comfortable rhythm. We went on a road trip, and suddenly I started feeling an upset stomach. We got home, and for several days, I just couldn't shake whatever it was that was making me feel sick and lightheaded. I went to the doctor, had some bloodwork done to check everything. At 42, it could be anything.

That evening, I got a phone call from my doctor. It was around 8:00pm - she called me from her cell phone. I was home alone when I received her call. When I heard her voice, my heart just sank, and I instantly thought the worst.

She said, "Are you sitting down?"

I said, "Yes."

She chuckled and said, "So you appear to be very pregnant!"

I yelled out, "WHAT? Are you sure? It can't be?"

She said, "Yes, your HCG levels are super high and we need to do more tests, but you are pregnant."

We hung up, and I'm just sitting there trying to think of how I was going to tell my husband, who was almost getting home, so I had to get myself together quick.

You know how Sarah laughed when the angel told her she'd have a baby in her old age? Genesis 18:14 asks, *"Is anything too hard for the Lord?"* At 42 with grown kids, I felt like I understood her disbelief.

Like, really, God? Now? After all these years of thinking that chapter was closed?

One thing I forgot to mention - my daughter was also pregnant at this time. She had just found out about two weeks earlier. She would be due the same time as me.

My husband comes in and I said, "So the doctor called."

He says, "And?"

I just looked at him and said, "We're going to have a baby!"

His mouth just dropped in disbelief.

We were so surprised, never thought that was the news we'd receive. So naturally, we're thinking all the things. We're too old. We've already had 4 kids, and they are all grown up. We're practically empty nesters.

***

As time went by, our mindset started to shift, and we transitioned to excitement! I pictured the baby room, the stroller, my daughter, and me being pregnant at the same time and sharing so many new first times.

Ecclesiastes 3:1-2 says, *"To everything there is a season, and a time to every purpose under the heaven: A time to be born, and a time to die."* I was so focused on the first part, planning and dreaming. God knew the whole verse would apply. He always knows the beginning from the end.

The months went by and I was doing all the routine appointments. One day, while I was at work, the doctor called and said I needed to do a test because one of my bloodwork tests came back abnormal. I started to cry and was overwhelmed with emotion and worry. I did the additional test that same week and had to wait over the weekend for results. That was the longest weekend of my life.

I kept thinking about Hannah in 1 Samuel 1:10, how she wept bitterly and prayed to the Lord. Hannah was praying FOR a child. I was praying to KEEP mine. Every kick, every movement felt precious and terrifying at the same time. Like holding water in your hands, knowing it's slipping through your fingers.

On Monday, they called me and my husband in to discuss. The specialist told us the baby was not developing as expected. The lungs are full of fluid and the brain - something something medical jargon. Long story short, we had to make a decision because the baby would be dependent on machines for the rest of its life or simply suffer.

When we left there, I had to drive alone because my husband went in his work vehicle. I got in my car, and I cried the whole way home - my heart was pierced! This song played on the radio called "Thy Will Be Done." I couldn't believe this was happening to me. I had so many questions! Like God, why me? Why us? I thought you loved me? I thought I was living an obedient life. I mean, the list goes on and on of all the things I felt!

That song hit my ears at that exact moment - coincidence? I think not. Matthew 26:39 shows Jesus in the garden praying, *"My Father, if it is possible, may this cup be taken from me. Yet not as I will, but as you will."* Even Jesus asked for another way. Even the Son of God said "if it's possible, can we not do this?" So my tears, my questions, my begging for a different outcome - I was in good company.

***

Life just keeps going around you like nothing happened. People are pumping gas, buying groceries, laughing at jokes, while your whole world just collapsed. It feels offensive, almost. Like, how dare the sun still shine when my heart is breaking?

My son Noah was born and went with the Lord on 10/18/16 at 9:45 p.m..

The name Noah means "rest" or "comfort." God gave me a son whose very name meant rest, and he went straight to eternal rest. Never knew struggle. Never knew pain. Never knew heartbreak. Straight from my womb to God's arms. Sometimes I wonder if that was mercy. A different kind than I wanted, but mercy nonetheless.

My grandson was born a week later on 10/28/16. Every year on his birthday, I look at him and think about how this is what Noah would look like if he were still here.

I went through labor pains and emotional pains at the same time. My spirit felt broken. Every day after that diagnosis, I would hold my tummy and savor the moments we had together. I would be changed forever.

2 Corinthians 1:3-4 calls *God "the Father of compassion and the God of all comfort, who comforts us in all our troubles."* God's comfort doesn't always feel comfortable. Sometimes it feels like barely surviving. Sometimes it feels like breathing when your lungs don't want to work. Sometimes comfort looks like making it through another hour when you didn't think you could make it through another minute.

Faith started to look and feel different. Everything I believed in and everything I thought I knew about myself was out the window. I thought my faith was rock solid until this journey! Why did God leave me? Why didn't he save Noah? These are the thoughts I had running through my head.

Job 13:15 says, "*Though he slay me, yet will I hope in him.*" I used to read that verse and think Job was so noble, so faithful. Now I know - it's desperation. It's having nowhere else to turn. It's realizing that even if God feels like your enemy, He's still your only hope. That's hanging-on-by-a-thread faith. And sometimes that's the most honest faith there is.

I kept thinking about Lazarus. Jesus KNEW he was dying. And He stayed where He was for two more days (John 11:6). When Jesus finally showed up, Martha said exactly what I was feeling: "*Lord, if you had been here, my brother would not have died*" (John 11:21). Translation: "*You could have prevented this. You chose not to. Why?*"

Romans 8:26 says, "*The Spirit helps us in our weakness. We do not know what we ought to pray for, but the Spirit himself intercedes for us through wordless groans.*" That was my prayer language during those days - groans too deep for words. When "why" was the only word I could manage. The Spirit was translating my pain into prayers I couldn't form.

The peace of God exists alongside pain. It's the hand that holds you while you weep. It's the presence that sits with you in the darkness. It's the whisper that reminds you that even this is still within His love.

My faith felt shattered, like glass dropped from a great height. Maybe that's what was needed to happen. Maybe my "rock solid" faith needed to break so God could rebuild it on His presence rather than my understanding of how life should work.

Even in my questions - "Why did God leave me? Why didn't He save Noah?" - I was still talking to Him. Even in my distress, I was still crying out to Him. And that's faith too. The raw, bleeding, desperate kind.

Habakkuk 3:17-18 became my heart's cry: *"Though the fig tree does not bud and there are no grapes on the vines, though the olive crop fails and the fields produce no food... yet I will rejoice in the Lord."* Everything was failing. My body was failing. My dreams were dying. My baby was gone. Yet... YET... that "yet" is where faith lives.

Jesus wept (John 11:35). The shortest verse in the Bible, and one of the most powerful. When Jesus arrived at Lazarus's tomb, even knowing He was about to raise him from the dead, He wept. God cries too. He grieved with me. He collected every tear (Psalm 56:8).

This loss marked me forever. It changed how I understood God, how I understood suffering, how I understood faith itself. Faith is continuing to seek God even when the questions have no answers. It's finding His peace while the storm rages around you.

My Uncle Ricky would call me often after this to remind me of how much God loved me and loves Noah. He would read scripture to me as anxiety had me paralyzed in grief. My Uncle Ricky, such a calm soul, has always known what to say to bring peace. He and Uncle Edwin were Messengers of His word when the days felt hard and heavy in my life! My mom kept reminding me, "You're gonna make it, Mari! EVERYTHING HAPPENS FOR A REASON," she gave me hope! My family and friends were the manifestation of a dream I had long ago of me in a bed surrounded by Angels around my bedside!

Because I AM saw it all. Because I AM felt it all. And Because I AM held me through it all.

Chapter 7

Medical Trauma & Healing – Buddy's Comfort

The day of the funeral when we went home after everyone had left, I wasn't feeling well. Something in me felt off, like my body was whispering a warning I couldn't understand. I lay down for just a minute, but when I pulled the blanket over me, it felt heavy and warm, too warm. When I touched the covers, they were drenched in blood. I froze. My heart sank into my stomach. I was hemorrhaging.

Everything that happened after felt like slow motion and fast-forward at the same time. My husband's voice panicked somewhere far away, my kids rushing in, towels, water running, the bathroom light blinding. They were trying to keep me in the tub so the blood wouldn't spill everywhere. It looked like a scene out of a movie, but this was no movie. This was my life, my body, my family's fear splashed across tile and porcelain.

My husband steadied his voice on the phone with 911 while our teenagers held me in the tub, doing anything to contain the blood.

The paramedics came. I remember their calm voices cutting through the chaos, hands on my wrist, the coldness creeping up my arms. I was fading. They lifted me onto the stretcher, and I heard one of them say, "She's losing a lot of blood."

At the hospital, they performed a quick procedure to stop the bleeding.

I whispered, "Jesus," and then everything went quiet.

There's a kind of quiet that isn't empty; it's crowded. Crowded with prayers you don't have words for, crowded with angels you can't see, crowded with the heavy breath of fear sitting on your chest and the lighter breath of God pressing back. Later, I thought of Romans 8:26, the Spirit Himself intercedes with groans too deep for words, and I realized that night I didn't need perfect prayers. I needed presence and I had it.

Somewhere inside that dark, Psalm 118:17 kept echoing like a stubborn drum: "I shall not die, but live, and declare the works of the Lord." Even when part of me wanted the pain to stop, something deeper kept choosing life.

***

They stopped the bleeding, but I was left weak, anemic, exhausted, pale as paper. For months, I moved like a ghost through the house, forcing smiles so my kids wouldn't see how bad it was. The tests finally gave the answer. Fibroids, tumors in my uterus. The doctor said, kindly but firmly, that a hysterectomy was the best option. I nodded like I understood, but inside I was screaming. It felt like another piece of womanhood being taken, another loss piled on top of what I'd already buried.

It felt as if my womb was grieving too. Pouring out what it had held, like my body was saying with me what words could not.

There's a grief nobody warns you about. It makes you feel for the version of yourself you thought you'd be. I grieved her in the laundry room, of all places, between a stack of towels and the hum of a machine that kept going when I didn't want to. I didn't have a psalm memorized for that moment, so I borrowed one: *"Even though I walk through the valley of the shadow of death, I will fear no evil, for You are with me."* (Psalm 23:4) I wasn't dying, but a shadow had definitely fallen. His with-me-ness kept my legs moving.

The surgery was scheduled for July 2020.

I said it to God plain: "So let me get this straight. You gave me a surprise at 42, took my baby, nearly let me bleed out, and now You're taking the womb that held him?" It felt like a second death. No more surprises. No more possibilities.

Over time, I began to hear Isaiah 54:1 differently, not as a taunt but a promise. There's another kind of fruitfulness God grows in desolate places. A motherhood that looks like comfort, prayer, presence.

***

March 2020. Before all of that, the world shut down. COVID was everywhere. I was working from home, disinfecting groceries like everyone else, trying to pretend normal existed. Funny how God moves ahead of us, setting things in place before we ever see the need. I wasn't a pet person. Never had been. My youngest daughter begged me constantly for a dog, but I was firm—*no*. I didn't want fur on my couch, hair on my clothes, or chewed shoes.

Then one random morning I woke up with this strange, stubborn thought: *Go hold a dog.*

I actually laughed out loud. "God, that can't be You. I can barely handle people right now, and You want me to hold a dog?"

But the nudge wouldn't go away. It felt gentle, persistent, the way God sometimes whispers when He knows we're too tired to listen any other way. So, I went. I drove to a local shelter, telling myself it was just curiosity. I didn't tell my family; I didn't want to give anyone false hope.

The moment they placed that little creature in my arms, my heart melted in a way I couldn't explain. He was soft, trembling, completely trusting. I didn't feel disgust. I felt peace.

I thought about how God fed Elijah by ravens when he was too spent to keep going (1 Kings 19). That day, I think He fed me by fur. Not dramatic or churchy; rather, soft and warm and exactly enough.

A week later, scrolling online late at night, I saw an ad for a puppy an hour away. I didn't think; I just felt that same pull. The next day, I packed everyone into the car without explanation. My husband thought we were driving to my dad's old house. When we pulled up to the dog store and my daughter saw the sign, she burst into tears. She knew.

They brought out this six-week-old ball of energy, and he ran straight to her, then to me, like he'd been waiting his whole little life for us. He was so full of love it felt unreal. We named him Buddy.

I don't have words for what shifted in me that day. God changed my heart. Me—the woman who once said, "Not in this house" was now cradling a puppy and crying like a kid.

Buddy became our heartbeat, our laughter, our new rhythm in a world gone strange. At the time, I thought he was just a quarantine distraction. But God was already preparing my medicine.

Sometimes the Lord answers prayers we haven't prayed yet. He tucks help into our tomorrow, then nudges us toward it. *"Before they call, I will answer; while they are still speaking, I will hear."* (Isaiah 65:24) I didn't know how sick my soul would feel. He did.

***

Then July came. The day of the surgery.

I remember shaking uncontrollably in the hospital waiting room. I could barely fill out the forms. My hands wouldn't stop trembling. The insurance office called—they had messed something up—and I thought maybe it was a sign. Maybe I should cancel. But the nurse called my name, and before I knew it, I was on the gurney.

I prayed, "Lord, if this is what I need to do to live, give me strength. But please, don't leave me."

The anesthesiologist's voice faded, and when I woke up, everything was different.

The pain was sharp, but the worst part was the heat—the fire crawling up my face and back. They said it was normal. "Medical menopause," the doctor explained casually, as if it were just another box to tick. But nothing about it felt normal. My heart raced. My mind spun. I couldn't calm down.

When I got home, it only got worse. Panic became my shadow. My nights turned into a series of heart-pounding episodes where I'd wake up drenched in sweat, gasping for air. I'd cry and shake and whisper, *"God, please, make it stop."* My husband didn't know what to do. My kids hovered, helpless.

People talk about faith like a switch you flip. Mine felt more like a dimmer I couldn't control. Some days it brightened; some nights it barely glowed. On the worst nights, I clung to Jesus' words, *"Come to Me, all you who are weary and burdened, and I will give you rest."* (Matthew 11:28) I wasn't looking for a sermon. I just wanted rest, more like a nap for my nervous system, or perhaps, a hush for my heart.

I felt insane. I remember looking in the mirror one morning and not recognizing the woman staring back at me. My body felt like it was betraying me. My faith felt like it was slipping away. I was alive, but barely living.

I'd walk around the house whispering, "JESUS, JESUS, JESUS," sometimes shouting it, clinging to that name like a rope in a storm. I thought about death more than I ever want to admit. I didn't want to die, I just didn't want to *feel* anymore.

Still feeling the loss of Noah, the emptiness of surgery, and the chaos inside my mind, I kept thinking, *This is it. This is how I'm going home.*

But even when my faith was hanging by a thread, God never let go.

I learned to breathe scripture more than recite it. *"When you pass through the waters, I will be with you; and through the rivers, they shall not overwhelm you."* (Isaiah 43:2) I wasn't drowning, but something was trying to pull me under. His with-you promise kept me afloat.

***

Buddy became my shadow. That dog refused to leave my side. He'd follow me from room to room like a tiny guardian. When I'd cry, he'd press his little head against my chest or lick my tears like he was trying to clean up my pain. It sounds silly, but sometimes I could swear God was using Buddy to talk to me.

One night, when I was at my lowest, I sat on the floor, rocking back and forth, whispering, "I can't do this anymore." Buddy climbed right into my lap, looked up at me, and let out this deep sigh. It was such a human sound it startled me. And in that second, peace flooded the room. Not the kind that fixes everything but one that says, *I'm still here.*

Isaiah 41:10 became my anthem: *"Do not fear, for I am with you; do not be dismayed, for I am your God. I will strengthen you and help you."*

Every panic attack, every night I couldn't sleep, I repeated that verse like a heartbeat. I didn't know it then, but my faith was rebuilding in those whispers.

There's a line in Philippians that started to make more sense to me: *"Be anxious for nothing… and the peace of God, which surpasses understanding, will guard your hearts and minds."* (Philippians 4:6–7) I always thought that meant the anxiety disappears. It didn't. But something stood guard. Peace took a shift at the door of my mind and refused to clock out.

Days turned into weeks. Some mornings I'd wake up and cry before my feet even hit the floor. But then I'd hear the sound of paws on the tile and that little tail wagging, and it gave me reason to stand up. Sometimes obedience to life looks like just feeding the dog.

Slowly, I started noticing small victories. I'd make it through a day without crying. I'd take a short walk. I'd laugh at a silly video. They were crumbs of light, but they were enough.

One morning, I stood in the kitchen and realized that I wasn't shaking. I wasn't dizzy. I was okay. Tears came again, but this time from gratitude.

And I heard another verse move through me like a breeze: *"Because of the Lord's great love we are not consumed… His mercies are new every morning."* (Lamentations 3:22–23) New. Every morning. I started looking for them, tiny mercies, like a scavenger hunt with God.

***

Months passed, and I started going to small gatherings again. Our women's group met at Panera once a week. One day, driving there, I was talking to God out loud like I often do. "Lord, do angels ever walk around like normal people?" I laughed at myself. "If they do, can I meet one today?"

We sat there sipping soup and talking about everything and nothing. Then I noticed a young man looking our way. Eventually, he walked up and said, "Can you pray for me?" He said he struggled with anxiety and wanted confidence in his walk with God. My heart nearly stopped. Anxiety, my old companion.

We prayed for him, all of us. Then he prayed for us. His words felt like balm poured over every raw place in my soul. When I opened my eyes, I felt lightheaded—but peaceful. I never saw him again. But I knew, deep in my spirit, that God had just answered my car-ride question.

Sometimes God sends reminders in human skin that He's close to the brokenhearted (Psalm 34:18). Sometimes He sends them in Panera, which is very on-brand for a Savior who shows up at wells and dinner tables and ordinary places where people gather because they're thirsty for something.

After that day, something changed. My panic didn't vanish overnight, but it lost its power. I started waking up before the alarm, not out of fear, but out of eagerness to see the sunrise.

I'd pour coffee, wrap up in a blanket, and sit on the porch with Buddy curled against my feet. I'd whisper, "Thank You for another morning." And I meant it.

Healing didn't come in one miraculous sweep. It came like sunrise… gradual, patient, soft.

I learned to stop measuring my healing by what hurt less and start measuring it by how much peace I let in.

Peace isn't passive. Jesus said, *"My peace I give to you… not as the world gives."* (John 14:27) The world hands you peace with a return policy. Jesus gives it with a lifetime guarantee. I started saying yes to that gift every day.

***

Sometimes I'd touch the scar on my abdomen and trace it with my fingers. I used to hate it, but now it felt like a signature—proof that God had brought me through. I'd look at myself in the mirror and say out loud, "I'm still here." And every time, Buddy's ears would perk up like he understood.

The Bible says our bodies are temples of the Holy Spirit. Mine had been cut open, stitched back together, scarred—but still holy. Still standing.

I thought of Paul's words: *"My grace is sufficient for you, for My power is made perfect in weakness."* (2 Corinthians 12:9) I don't like weakness. I don't like needing help. But there's a strange relief in letting grace be enough when I'm not.

The more I thought about it, the more I realized that healing wasn't about getting back to who I used to be. It was about becoming someone new—someone who didn't just believe God existed but had felt Him in the fire and survived.

Every night before bed, I still whisper Isaiah 41:10. Not out of fear anymore, but gratitude. Because now I know that peace doesn't mean the absence of pain, it means the presence of God *in* it.

***

Looking back, I understand why God sent Buddy before the storm. He knew I'd need something tangible to remind me of love when everything else felt empty. He knew I'd need a reason to smile when I couldn't pray. God always sends help ahead of time. Sometimes it comes in the form of people. Sometimes it comes with paws.

Psalm 34:18 says, *"The Lord is close to the brokenhearted and saves those who are crushed in spirit."* That verse became real to me in fur and warm eyes and quiet company.

I can't tell you the exact day the anxiety faded. It just… softened. The edges dulled. I could breathe again. I could laugh without guilt. I could sleep through the night.

I used to ask God why He let me walk through so many waters. Now I see the pattern. Not the pain, never the pain, but the presence. "I will never leave you nor forsake you." (Hebrews 13:5) I stitched that promise into my daily life like a hidden hem. It held me together when I felt like unraveling.

Now, when people ask how I made it through, I tell them about a season when my world was falling apart and God rebuilt it piece by piece. I tell them about nights I walked the hall whispering "Jesus" until morning came. I tell them about a scar that doesn't ache anymore and a dog that taught me how to feel safe again.

Healing didn't come through medicine alone. It came through mercy.

God didn't rush me. He sat with me.

And through it all, I realized something simple yet profound. Sometimes the miracle isn't that the storm stops, it's that you're still standing when it passes.

Buddy still follows me everywhere, and every time he curls beside me, I remember that season. It doesn't haunt me anymore. It humbles me.

Because I know now, peace isn't found when everything's perfect. It's found when you finally believe that even in your weakest moment, God never leaves.

He was there through the blood and the fear. Through the panic and the prayers. Through every "I can't do this" and every breath that followed anyway.

He was there—in the stillness, in the whisper, in the wag of a little tail.

And I'm still here, too.

Because He is.

I think about one last promise when the house is quiet and Buddy is a warm weight by my feet: *"You keep track of all my sorrows. You have collected all my tears in Your bottle."* (Psalm 56:8) Mine must be a whole shelf by now. But none of them were wasted. Not one.

And in the morning, when the light edges the blinds and the coffee sighs and Buddy thumps his tail against the floor, I say it again, like a declaration and a prayer, "Thank You. I'm still here."

Chapter 8

Father's Passing & Grief

Just living life, pressing forward. I was still dealing with an unexplained sickness. Every day was like a precious pearl, just trying to care for that temple. My Dad was going through medical issues, and most of the time, he understood how I was feeling. We had this unspoken bond, both of us fighting battles in our bodies that doctors couldn't quite name. He'd look at me across the dinner table with eyes that said, "I get it, Mija. Keep going."

My father had always been a fighter. Even after years of struggling with his own issues, even after the divorce when I was young, he found his way back to us. He became the grandfather my kids needed. Redemption looks different for everyone, but for my Dad, it looked like showing up. Day after day. Year after year. Making up for lost time with presence.

***

March 12, 2025. The date is burned into my memory like a scar. My Dad wakes up and says he's not feeling well. He felt bloated and had a ringing in his ear. He was often feeling off. He was 74 years young at this point, and so we took him to the hospital just to make sure it wasn't anything serious. I remember I was at a work meeting, and my husband drove my Dad to the hospital. He called me and said you have to leave work and come, it's serious.

The drive to the hospital felt like moving through water. Everything slowed down. The radio played some song about hope, and I wanted to throw my phone out the window. When I got there, the doctors told me my Dad needed open heart surgery. He had 4 clogged arteries. In disbelief, I just felt like this was a nightmare. How is this possible? My Dad was always on top of his medical care, and none of the doctors ever mentioned heart issues. This explained so much of why he wasn't feeling well.

The doctor's words echoed in my head: "If we don't operate soon, he won't make it through the month." My legs turned to water. I had to grab the wall to stay upright. Ecclesiastes 3:2 whispered in my spirit: *"A time to be born and a time to die,"* but I pushed it away. Not yet. Not my Dad. Not now.

Surgery was scheduled for 3 days out. My heart was in my stomach, and my nerves were a mess. I couldn't eat. I felt so sick from my anxiety. I had to keep it together; I had to be strong for him. That night, I went to his room and found him staring at the ceiling. "Mija," he said softly, "if something happens—" I cut him off. "Nothing's going to happen, Papi. You're going to be fine." But we both knew. We both knew that sometimes love means pretending to be brave when you're terrified.

I prayed and cried and prayed and sobbed and even yelled out loud. *God, what are you doing?? I need you, God!!* I felt I was slowly dying. Being sick and still working on myself, how could these events be taking place now? Why now?

The morning of his surgery, I anointed his forehead with oil I'd brought from home. As they wheeled him away, he grabbed my hand. "I love you, Mija." Those words hung in the air long after he disappeared behind the operating room doors. Something in his eyes looked like goodbye.

***

My Dad got the surgery. He's trying to recover, but complications. One after another! His kidneys started failing. Then an infection set in. I kept praying and believing God was going to show up. I'll serve You better. I'll pray more. I'll fast. Just please, don't take my father."

A month went by, and he was still in the trauma center of the hospital. I sat with him from morning til night, waiting for some change.

His hands, once so strong, now looked fragile as bird bones. I played music for him – old Spanish songs. I put on some scriptures on my phone for him. He was out of it, on a trachea and unable to talk. But sometimes, when I'd read Psalm 23, I'd see a tear roll down his cheek. He was still in there, fighting.

I brought things from home to make his room feel less sterile. His favorite blanket. Pictures of the grandkids. The cologne he always wore - just a tiny spray on his pillow so he could smell something familiar. The nurses thought I was crazy, but I didn't care. If my Dad was going to fight this battle, he wasn't going to fight it alone in some cold, impersonal room.

We were on month two, and no change. The doctors started having different conversations. Words like "quality of life" and "difficult decisions" floated around. I wanted to cover my ears like a child and scream until they stopped talking. This wasn't how the story was supposed to end. We were supposed to have more time. More Sunday dinners. More terrible dad jokes. More everything.

Everyone came to talk to me at the hospital, and the decision was made after he flatlined twice. The first time, they brought him back in 3 minutes. The second time, it took 7. The doctor pulled me aside. "Each time takes something from him," he said gently. "His brain, his organs - they can't keep doing this." I understood what he was saying, but understanding and accepting are two different things entirely.

I went outside and just began to sob. My heart was breaking! I felt I was living a nightmare! The hospital courtyard had this little garden with a bench. I sat there in the dark, looking up at stars I couldn't see through the city lights, and I wrestled with God like Jacob.

Again, my faith was tested. Again, I needed to trust God! Again, I was faced with loss! Again, the pain was so unbearable that I could barely breathe. I just kept saying his name: Jesus, Jesus, Jesus!!

That night, I stayed in his room. I held his hand and told him every memory I could think of. The day he walked me down the aisle.

How proud he looked when he held his first grandchild. I told him it was okay to let go, that we would be okay, even though I didn't believe it myself. Giving someone permission to die when everything in you screams for them to stay - that's a special kind of agony.

I didn't want my Dad to suffer anymore! He went through so much these 2 months in the hospital. Procedures, tubes, needles, machines – they'd turned my strong father into something I didn't recognize. His body was there, but he was already halfway to heaven.

It was late, 5 AM, and I couldn't close my eyes. I was at home, but my spirit was still in that hospital room. I was just praying, *God, please don't let my Dad suffer anymore, Lord, please!* I kept saying this over and over! The words became a rhythm, like a heartbeat, like breathing.

The phone rang, and it startled me. It was the nurse. My heart sank! The words I dreaded to hear! She said, "Sweety, I'm so sorry, your Dad passed at 5:01 AM. May 2, 2025."

The world stopped. I mean, literally, everything just stopped. The clock on the wall, the birds outside, my heart - everything froze for a moment. Then it all came crashing down at once. My Dad, absent in the body but present with the Lord!

***

I was left with a flushing of memories, pain, and brokenness! The coffee cup he always used, still sitting in the kitchen. His reading glasses on the nightstand. The indent in his favorite chair. All these pieces of a life, but no life to fill them.

I quickly said, "Thank you, God! Thank you that my Dad is not in pain anymore," but my flesh felt so selfish because I just missed him! The gratitude and the grief got all tangled up together, and I couldn't separate them. I was relieved he wasn't suffering and devastated he was gone. Both things were true at the same time.

I would never be the same! Watching my Dad decompose in front of me was the most life-changing experience of my life! There's something about watching strength become weakness, watching someone who carried you become someone you have to carry. It rewrites everything you thought you knew about life and death and everything in between.

The funeral was a blur. People said nice things. Everyone meant well. But all I could think about was how none of them saw what I saw. Those two months in the hospital. The way hope slowly leaked out of the room. The gradual goodbye that no one prepares you for. They saw the end result. I lived the process.

I dove into the Word looking for peace! The grief made me desperate for God in a way I'd never been before. *Lazarus, get up, Lazarus!* I kept reading that story over and over. Jesus wept. Jesus knew Lazarus would rise, and still, He wept. That gave me permission to cry even while believing in resurrection.

I envisioned God calling my Father from that bed. Calling his name into Heaven with him! That filled me with joy! Even till the end of age, God is with us! I imagined my Dad taking that first breath in heaven – no tubes, no machines, just pure, clean air. I imagined him running. He hadn't been able to run in years.

I thought about this scripture immediately: 1 Corinthians 2:9 - "*However, as it is written: 'What no eye has seen, what no ear has heard, and what no human mind has conceived' - the things God has prepared for those who love him.*"

Whatever my Dad was experiencing now, it was beyond my comprehension. Beyond the hospital beds and heart monitors. Beyond the suffering. He was seeing colors that don't exist here. Hearing music we can't imagine. Whole and healed and home.

I'm now learning how temporary this life is. God stands outside of time and is with us! Seventy-four years. It sounds like a long time until it's over. Then it feels like a breath, a whisper, a single heartbeat in eternity's rhythm.

I think about how all the disciples died unthinkable deaths, and they were called the chosen of Jesus! Pain is a part of the process! Peter was crucified upside down. Paul beheaded. John boiled in oil (though he survived). They didn't get easy endings. They got glorious ones. There's a teaching that comes from the spirit that impairs our vision when we focus on the struggle and not the glory!

Romans 8:18 - *"For I consider that the sufferings of this present time are not worthy to be compared with the glory that is to be revealed to us."*

This verse used to be just words. Now it's an anchor. My Dad's suffering – those terrible two months – they're not even a speck compared to where he is now. If I could ask him if it was worth it, if the pain was worth the glory, I know what he'd say. He'd laugh that laugh of his and say, "Mija, you have no idea."

Two months ago, if you had asked me if I could get through this, I would've said no way! I would probably die of a heart attack. I felt so weak. But God! He gave me the strength I needed to get through this season!

2 Corinthians 12:9 became real: *"My grace is sufficient for you, for my power is made perfect in weakness."* I didn't have strength. I borrowed His. Every day I showed up at that hospital, every decision I had to make, every moment I didn't fall apart – that wasn't me. That was grace. Pure grace.

Don't you see how the grief comes in waves? Sometimes I'm fine, laughing at something, living my life, and then I'll smell his cologne in a store, or I'll hear someone call their dad "Papi," and I'm right back in that hospital room. Grief isn't linear. It's a circle that keeps coming around, each time a little different but always familiar.

This gave birth to an urgency in me to share God's truth! To my kids, to everyone around me! Life is so uncertain and goes by so quickly! I started having conversations I'd been putting off. I started saying "I love you" more. I started treating every gathering like it might be the last because now I knew – it might be.

I find myself asking God to open my eyes to see and open my ears to hear what the Spirit is calling me to do! There's a clarity that comes with loss. Suddenly, all the stupid things you worried about seem so small. The grudges, the petty arguments, the wasted time – none of it matters when you're standing at a graveside.

God uses what is meant to break us to build us! The same grief that brought me to my knees also brought me to His feet. The same loss that emptied me also made room for Him to fill me with something new. Purpose from pain. Beauty from ashes. The great exchange Isaiah talks about.

I received so much support from friends and family! My church family showed up in ways I didn't expect. Meals appeared at my door. People sat with me in silence when words weren't enough. They didn't try to fix it or explain it. They just were present. Sometimes presence is the best present.

My Dad's passing shattered any remaining illusions I had about doing life alone. Grief this heavy wasn't meant to be carried in isolation. I finally understood that the body of Christ meant that we need each other, not as a nice idea, but as survival.

Galatians 6:2 says, *"Carry each other's burdens, and in this way, you will fulfill the law of Christ."* I learned to let people carry me when I couldn't walk. I learned that accepting help isn't weakness; it's wisdom. I learned that we were never meant to grieve alone.

I say this humbly to help those who need to allow themselves to be loved. Because there was a time I felt alone and disconnected, and didn't mind being there because the pain of letting anyone in and rejecting me would be far more to deal with. But you know what I learned? I learned that the pain of isolation is worse than the risk of rejection. Every time.

My Dad's death taught me things his life couldn't. It taught me that love transcends death. Those memories are treasures no one can steal. Sometimes the greatest act of love is letting go. And God is closest when we're most broken.

I still talk to him sometimes, not in a weird way, but in a daughterly way. I tell him about my day. About the grandkids. I know he can't answer, but somehow, I feel heard. Maybe that's crazy. Or maybe that's just how love works – it keeps reaching even when the person is beyond reach.

Psalm 34:18 promises, *"The Lord is near to the brokenhearted and saves the crushed in spirit."* Near. Not distant. Not watching from heaven. Near. In the tears. In the memories. In the quiet moments when the grief feels too heavy to carry.

Some days I'm angry. Angry at myself for all the time we wasted. The anger is part of it, too. It's not pretty or spiritual, but it's honest. And I think God prefers honest anger to fake peace.

What I know now is that grief is love with nowhere to go. It's all the love you still have for someone, but they're not here to receive it. So it sits in your chest, heavy and aching, looking for an outlet. Sometimes it comes out as tears. Sometimes, when you remember something funny they did. And sometimes, as a service, when you do something kind in their memory.

My father's passing didn't just take him from this world; it changed my entire understanding of what holds value. Every sunrise feels more precious. Every phone call with my mom feels more important. Every moment with my children feels more urgent. Death has a way of sharpening life, making everything more vivid, more immediate, more sacred.

The last thing he ever said to me was, "I love you, Mari."

Because "I AM" – because God is still God even in grief, even in loss, even in the valley of the shadow of death – I can keep walking. Not because I'm strong, but because He is. Not because I understand, but because I trust. Not because the pain is gone, but because His presence is greater than my pain.

My Dad is home. Really home. Not the home with the leaky roof and the squeaky door, but the home we're all longing for, whether we know it or not. The home where nothing breaks, nothing dies, nothing ends. And someday, because of "I AM," I'll see him there. Until then,

I carry him with me – in my memories, in my heart, in the way I love others because he taught me how.

Romans 8:18 remains true: *"For I consider that the sufferings of this present time are not worthy to be compared with the glory that is to be revealed to us."* The suffering was real and so was the loss. But the glory – oh, the glory that awaits – that's the most real thing of all.

Chapter 9

Just leave it as Forgiveness & Redemption

You know, I thought I had already made peace with my husband when I walked away from him all those years ago. I thought teaching my kids to forgive as Christ forgave us was the end of that story. I thought we were done. But God had one more chapter to write that I never saw coming.

Years went by. He wasn't involved much in the kids' lives. It was later in life that he tried to grow those broken relationships with his kids. I taught my kids to forgive as Christ has forgiven us, over and over. It was hard for them, but they understood and slowly started letting him in. It wasn't without a battle. He was fighting his demons and never felt worthy or accepted. I could understand why he felt that way. His choices led him down that path.

Till this day, I was never in a place of hating him, though I had so many reasons to fall into that. I never shut the door on him being able to father his children. He just chose not to.

I want you to understand that. Because when people hear what happened, they assume I must have hated him. That all those years of hurt and abuse and abandonment must have turned into bitterness. But it didn't. And I can't take credit for that because that was God's work in me. That was years of choosing forgiveness, even when it didn't feel good and made little sense.

Colossians 3:13 says, *"Bear with each other and forgive one another if any of you has a grievance against someone. Forgive as the Lord forgave you."* I had grievances. Oh boy, did I have grievances. But that verse doesn't say "forgive when you feel like it" or "forgive when they deserve it." It says forgive *as* the Lord forgave you. And how did He forgive me? Completely. Unconditionally. Before I even asked.

So that became my standard. Not my feelings. Not whether he deserved it. But how Christ forgave me.

Recently, when I came back from vacation, which was in June 2024, he left me a voicemail, "I need someone to talk to."

My heart sank because it's not like we talked at all. We hadn't had a real conversation in years. Maybe a text here and there about the kids, but nothing substantial. Hearing his voice on that voicemail, there was something different about it. Something desperate.

The day I came back from vacation, I called him. I prayed before calling because he had bipolar tendencies, and you never knew what you were going to get.

I sat in my car before I dialed. I needed a moment. I needed to talk to God first. "Lord, I don't know what this is about. I don't know what he needs. Please guard my heart. Give me wisdom. Let Your words flow through me, not mine."

My hands were shaking a little when I pressed call, more out of uncertainty… anticipation. I didn't know what to expect. Would he be angry? Manipulative? Or was this something else?

We were on the phone for about an hour. He begged me to forgive him for all the times he made me suffer. For not being a good dad. For not being a good husband.

An hour. A whole hour. And the man on the other end wasn't the man I remembered. He wasn't defensive or making excuses. He was broken. And he was taking responsibility for things I never thought he'd acknowledge.

He went through everything. The abuse. The abandonment. The years he wasn't there. The ways he failed as a father. The ways he failed as a husband. And he didn't just list them, he was morose about them.

I told him I had no grudges against him. I forgave him a long time ago.

And what shocked me was the fact that when I said those words, I meant them. They weren't just something I said to be nice or to get him off the phone. They were true. Somewhere along the journey, through all those years of choosing forgiveness daily, it had actually happened. I had truly forgiven him.

And it wasn't even a shallow kind where you just don't think about it anymore. Or the fake kind where you say "it's fine," but you're still carrying the hurt. It was so real. Like God, has any emotion been more real?

Matthew 18:21–22 talks about this. Peter asked Jesus, *"Lord, how many times shall I forgive my brother or sister who sins against me? Up to seven times?"* Jesus answered, *"I tell you, not seven times, but seventy-seven times."*

I used to think that was just a big number Jesus threw out there. But now I understand that means continual choice rather than a big figure. Every time a memory surfaces. Every time you see the impact of their choices on your children. Every time the wound tries to reopen. You forgive again. And again. And again.

I'd lost count of how many times I'd had to choose forgiveness. But each time made the next time a little easier. Not because the hurt was less, but because the habit of forgiveness was stronger.

I told him God loved him, to seek Him out, and He would help with whatever struggles he had. He asked me to mail him a Bible. I said, "Of course. You have to believe that God is with you, call on His name."

A Bible. The man who had slammed me against a wall. The man who made me feel worthless. The man who abandoned his children. That man was asking me to send him a Bible.

And you know what? Without a second of hesitation, I said yes.

That's what grace does. It makes you say yes when everything in your flesh wants to say no. It makes you extend help to people who hurt you. It makes you a vessel of God's love to the most unlikely people.

Isaiah 61:1–3 talks about binding up the brokenhearted, proclaiming freedom for captives, comforting those who mourn. That's what I was doing in that moment. Not because I'm some super-Christian, but because God's grace was flowing through me to reach someone who needed it desperately.

I said a little prayer for him... He brought up past times when we were young and told me he loves his kids. He said he was having complications with his heart, and I could sense the fear in his voice about his condition. I told him not to fear, that God would be with him. He kept begging for forgiveness, and we ended our call with a peaceful, "Take it easy."

His words undid me. I'd seen him angry more times than I could count. I'd seen him distant, cold, manipulative. But vulnerable? Broken? Seeking God? This was new territory.

And in his brokenness, I saw what God must see when He looks at all of us…beloved children who have lost their way. People desperate for grace they don't deserve. Broken people who need a Savior.

Romans 2:4 says that *"God's kindness is intended to lead you to repentance."* Maybe all those years of me refusing to hate him, of keeping the door cracked open, of praying for him even when it seemed pointless, maybe all of that was God's kindness working through me. Slowly and patiently, drawing him toward repentance.

The conversation ended with "take it easy." Simple, casual words. But there was peace in them. A sense of closure, or maybe a new beginning. I didn't know which.

That was the last time I would hear his voice. On July 19, 2024, our son's birthday, he took his own life and his wife's life.

When I write those words, they still don't feel real. How do you go from seeking God to… that? How do you go from asking for a Bible to ending not just your life, but someone else's?

His brother called me with the news. I dropped the phone, and in tears, I felt a part of me die that day. I felt so broken for his wife's family and his three other children. I didn't understand why this was happening…we prayed.

The phone hit the floor. I heard his brother's voice still talking, but I couldn't pick it up. I couldn't move. My body just… stopped.

We just prayed together. He just asked for a Bible. He was guilty of his sins and asked for forgiveness. How could this be the ending?

Where was the redemption arc I expected? Where was the story of him turning his life around, building relationships with his kids, becoming the father he should have been? Where was the happy ending?

But I'm learning, painfully, that God's redemption doesn't always look like our redemption. Sometimes the rescue happens in ways we can't see. Sometimes the healing takes place on the other side of heaven.

I had to drive to my daughter's house and deliver the news that her father had taken his life and his wife's. My son was traveling to California, so we had to wait for him to arrive to tell him. So many mixed emotions, not only about what he did, but about how my kids would process that their father did this.

That drive…I don't even remember most of it. I was on autopilot. My mind was racing with a thousand thoughts and being completely blank at the same time.

How do you tell your children this? What words do you use? How do you explain that their father, who they were just starting to let back in, who was just starting to try, made a choice that ended everything?

How do I speak life into my kids? How do I speak obedience and remind them of God's word that demands forgiveness? The wound is too fresh. This is going to take time.

The command to forgive felt almost cruel in that moment. God, how? How do you forgive someone for this? For making our son's birthday forever associated with death? For traumatizing my children in ways that will take years. maybe decades, to heal? For taking an innocent woman's life?

But even as I wrestled with these impossible questions, I knew unforgiveness would only add more weight to the tragedy. It would be like drinking poison and expecting him to die. The only person imprisoned by my bitterness would be me and my children, if they followed my example.

Ephesians 4:31–32 became my roadmap: *"Get rid of all bitterness, rage and anger, brawling and slander, along with every form of malice. Be kind and compassionate to one another, forgiving each other, just as in Christ God forgave you."*

Notice what it doesn't say. It doesn't say "Get rid of bitterness when you feel like it" or "Be compassionate when the person deserves it." It says get rid of it. Period. And forgive just as Christ forgave you, which means completely and at great cost.

I remember a couple of weeks before this happened, I had a dream of him and his wife standing in my bedroom. It startled me. It made no sense, but I prayed for her and I prayed for him. I didn't know what to pray, so I asked the Holy Spirit to intervene.

Romans 8:26 says, *"In the same way, the Spirit helps us in our weakness. We do not know what we ought to pray for, but the Spirit himself intercedes for us through wordless groans."*

The Holy Spirit knew what was coming. He gave me that dream. He prompted me to pray. And even though the outcome wasn't what I hoped, I trust those prayers mattered. Maybe they brought moments of peace I'll never know about. Maybe they created opportunities for repentance in those final days. Maybe they'll matter in eternity in ways I can't comprehend from here.

Now that they are gone, I made a promise as a mother to keep praying for her children every day as if I were praying for my own kids.

Tragedy struck again. We're just trying to understand.

Her children, his wife's children, are now motherless because of the choices my ex-husband made. Three more kids added to my daily prayer list. Kids who will grow up with a wound I can't heal, with questions I can't answer, with a loss that shouldn't have happened.

How do I pray for them? What do I even say? But this is what love looks like. This is what it means to be the body of Christ. We carry each other's burdens. We show up for people even when we're barely holding ourselves together.

James 5:16 says, *"Therefore confess your sins to each other and pray for each other so that you may be healed. The prayer of a righteous person is powerful and effective."*

My prayers for these children might be the only bridge they have to understanding that not all adults abandon you. That God's love remains, even when human love fails catastrophically. That there's still hope in the darkest valleys.

I was angry at my ex-husband, but I wasn't angry if that makes sense.

I know that sounds contradictory. How can you be angry but not angry at the same time? But it's the truth. I was angry at what he did. At the devastation he left behind. At the ripple effects that will last for generations. At the fact that he took someone else with him.

But angry at him as a person? At his soul? No. Because all I could see was a broken man who never found the healing he desperately needed. A man who fought demons I'll never fully understand. A man who, in his darkest moment, made a choice that couldn't be undone.

That's the mystery of Christian forgiveness that it creates space for righteous anger at sin while extending grace to the sinner. Jesus demonstrated this perfectly. He overturned tables in the temple, in righteous anger at the corruption. But from the cross, He prayed, *"Father, forgive them, for they do not know what they are doing"* (Luke 23:34).

I prayed in despair, *Lord, let him be forgiven.* How could I pray a prayer like this when her children have no mother today? I can't explain it. How does someone get beaten for years and not hate the person? I can't explain it, but that was my life for a long time.

People ask me all the time, How do you not hate him? How do you pray for his forgiveness after everything he did, especially now?

Honestly, I can't fully explain it using human logic. It doesn't make sense in my flesh. But 1 John 4:19 does explain it: *"We love because He first loved us."*

My capacity to forgive doesn't come from my goodness or strength. It comes from being loved by a God who forgave me for things I didn't deserve forgiveness for. Every time I extend grace to my ex-husband, even now, even after this, I'm simply passing on what's been given to me.

This is the scandal of the Gospel. Romans 5:8 says, *"But God demonstrates His own love for us in this: While we were still sinners, Christ died for us."* He didn't wait for us to get our act together or to deserve it, for that matter. He loved us in our mess, and it is this love that transforms us.

Because "I AM," says the Lord.

We don't need to know all the details; we just need to trust that God works for the good of those who love Him.

This is the anchor that keeps me from spiraling into despair. Because "I AM" – the eternal, unchanging, sovereign God – is still on the throne. Because He's faithful even when we're faithless. Because He can bring beauty from ashes and joy from mourning.

Romans 8:28 isn't just a nice verse anymore. It's a lifeline I'm holding with both hands: *"And we know that in all things God works for the good of those who love Him, who have been called according to His purpose."*

Notice it doesn't say all things are good. This situation isn't good. What he did wasn't good. The devastation left behind isn't good. But God works all things, even this unspeakable tragedy, for good for those who love Him.

I think about Joseph's story in Genesis. His brothers sold him into slavery. He was falsely accused and thrown in prison. Years of suffering and injustice. But at the end, in Genesis 50:20, he tells his brothers, *"You intended to harm me, but God intended it for good, to accomplish what is now being done, the saving of many lives."*

The enemy intended this tragedy to destroy our family, fill us with bitterness, make us question God's goodness, and to shatter our faith. But God intends to use it for good. I don't know how yet. I can't see the full picture. But I trust Him.

Every time the memory creeps in of the day he spat in my face as if I was garbage to him, the feeling returns. It was the lowest form of rejection. I was 17 and pregnant, and in that moment, I thought about Jesus about *Matthew 5:39 "But I say unto you, That ye resist not evil: but whosoever shall smite thee on thy right cheek, turn to him the other also."* I didn't feel my pain but I felt pity for him. What must be happening inside you to make you treat another human that way?

In trusting God, I realize that forgiveness isn't a feeling. It's a decision and a choice I make every single day, sometimes every single hour.

It's a choice I made when I first walked away from the abuse. A choice I made every time a memory surfaced. A choice I made when teaching my kids about grace. A choice I made during that phone call in June. And a choice I'm still making now…after everything.

I'll probably have to keep making this choice for the rest of my life. Every July 19th when our son's birthday rolls around. Every time I see the long-term effects on my children. Every time someone asks me about their father. Every time the "what ifs" creep in.

But I'm willing to make that choice. Because unforgiveness is a prison, and I refuse to live there. Because I want to model for my children what it looks like to trust God when nothing makes sense. Because I believe, and I have to believe, that God's grace is sufficient, His power is made perfect in weakness, and His love never fails.

Hebrews 12:15 warns us: *"See to it that no one falls short of the grace of God and that no bitter root grows up to cause trouble and defile many."*

Bitterness is like a root system. It grows underground where you can't see it. It spreads and ultimately chokes out everything good.

It poisons you AND everyone connected to you. I've seen bitterness destroy families, churches, friendships, whatnot. I've watched people become consumed by it.

I refuse to let that root take hold in my heart or in my children's hearts.

So I choose forgiveness. It's not easy, no. If truth be told, it is the hardest thing I've ever done. But I did it nonetheless. Why? Because he deserved? I highly doubt that. Or you think that the pain is gone? Nope, pain never really goes, does it? So let me tell you, I forgave him because I've been forgiven much, and to whom much has been forgiven, much is required.

This is my testimony: Even in the darkest valleys, even when forgiveness seems impossible, even when tragedy strikes and nothing makes sense, God is still good. His love still transforms. His grace still abounds. His promises still hold.

Because "I AM" lives…because the great I AM is still God…I can forgive. I can heal. I can hope again!

The story isn't over. My ex-husband's life ended in tragedy, but God's story continues. In my children, in his wife's children, and in everyone touched by this pain.

And one day, when I see Jesus face to face, I believe I'll understand. I'll see how He wove even this thread of darkness into a tapestry of redemption. I'll see how the prayers mattered. I'll see how the forgiveness freed both me and him.

Until then, I walk by faith, not by sight. I choose forgiveness, not feelings. I cling to the "I AM," not to my understanding.

Because He is faithful, and that suffices.

Chapter 10

Friendship & Community in Faith

For so long, I thought strength meant standing alone. I thought protecting myself meant building walls so high that no one could climb them. But isolation isn't protection; instead, it's a prison of our own making. And God, in His infinite wisdom and patience, kept sending people to knock on those walls until I finally had the courage to let them in.

1 Corinthians 12:12 says, *"Just as a body, though one, has many parts, but all its many parts form one body, so it is with Christ."* I read that verse a hundred times before I really understood it. We weren't meant to do this alone, nor were we designed for isolation. We were created for community, connection and for the beautiful mess of doing life together.

So, I decided to see a therapist. I prayed about this and I knew God was going to find me someone I felt comfortable with. My friends said you don't always find the "one" on your first try but I was hopeful. I was assigned a therapist, and on our first meeting, I instantly felt the connection. I felt heard and understood. She felt so genuine and knowledgeable. She offered ways for me to deal with the anxiety.

One thing I loved was that she never once said anything about medication; she offered ways to process what was happening to me. One phrase she taught me, which I still think about to this day, was "NO STINKIN THINKIN"! Her words were imprinted in my brain. I'm so thankful to God for her! Therapy has been a blessing!

Sometimes God puts people in our path who aren't just counselors but angels in disguise. Proverbs 11:14 tells us, *"Where there is no guidance, a people falls, but in an abundance of counselors there is safety.*" My therapist became part of my abundance of counselors, part of my safety net that God was weaving around me.

I was still looking for ways to connect outside of home, so one day, when I woke up, I decided to look at my church website for a group I could possibly join.

I felt I had to reconnect myself. God was telling me to tear the walls down that I had built for myself.

When I went on the website, there were quite a few groups to choose from. I didn't know who to pick. So I didn't pick any. I went to bed and asked God to point me to the group he wants me to be a part of. The next day, I revisited the website and found this women's group; I think it was called Bible Walkers. They do a bible study and also go for a walk before the study. I thought that was cool cause I need some exercise. I joined the group.

On my first day attending, I almost didn't make it; I was so nervous with anxiety. I prayed so much cause I really wanted to go. I got in the car and went. I took something for my stomach just in case. When I got there, I met the leader, who was so nice that I instantly felt good about this. It was four ladies, and we started walking around the little lake.

I started talking to one of the ladies and she was sharing with me how she lost her husband a few years ago. She battled cancer and was doing much better. The next lady I met also shared how she had lost her Dad and was dealing with that loss. And my Leader had also lost a daughter. I mean, these ladies were all warriors in my eyes!

I wondered why I was meeting people who suffered from losses and were dealing with grief. I thought it was cause they would understand my pain of losing Noah. God doesn't make mistakes, and this felt like a Divine Appointment. Later on, you'll see why God put me in this specific group. The things they shared made me feel like I wasn't alone. Like how strong they were gave me hope that maybe I can get to the other side of this. They gave me so much hope that I started to feel a light I haven't seen in a while. When I went home that night, I cried the whole way at how good God is and how he sent me to this specific group. These women were like God sent! I felt so grateful!

Hebrews 10:24–25 came alive in those moments: *"And let us consider how we may spur one another on toward love and good deeds, not giving up meeting together, as some are in the habit of doing, but encouraging one another—and all the more as you see the Day approaching."* These women didn't just walk with me around a lake, but they did so through the valley of the shadow of death. They showed me that grief doesn't have to be carried alone and healing happens in community. I realized sometimes the best ministry is simply showing up and saying, "Me too. I've been there. You're going to make it."

***

It's been a process. It took some time to break what I was going through. Every time I was planning to go to our Thursday night sessions, I would somehow get sick out of nowhere. It was like an attack on me physically. I didn't want to stop going but I was afraid of feeling so terrible.

My spirit is so sensitive to energy around me. I've been like this since I was young. This isn't something new! What is new is that I recognize the fear behind it. I hate feeling this way! But I'm gonna thrive, I'm gonna defeat this! I kept going and attending. And every time I went, what a powerful time it was! I can't think of one time that I wasn't touched by the spirit! I learned and listened and opened my heart and broke down those walls to receive all God has for me!

The enemy knows that isolated believers are vulnerable believers. He knows that when we're alone, we're easier targets for his lies and attacks. That's why he fought so hard to keep me from that group. But James 4:7 promises, *"Submit yourselves, then, to God. Resist the devil, and he will flee from you."* Every Thursday that I showed up despite feeling sick, every time I pushed through the anxiety to be with my sisters in Christ, I was resisting. I was declaring that the community was worth fighting for.

***

There is one specific time I remember, We met at Panera Bread like we normally did. On the drive there, I remember asking God if Angels exist, like walking around us like regular people. I was in my thoughts, like asking God funny things. I always talk to God, imagining him being humorous. I even said God, can I meet an Angel? I shook my head like Maribel, you are such a nut!!

I walk into Panera and meet the ladies. We were sitting talking, it was like 3 of us, I think, on this day. I felt someone staring at me while the ladies and I were talking. After a while, this young fellow walks up to me and says, Can I ask you for a prayer? The ladies and I were like, of course. I said to him; What do you need prayer for? He said, I suffer from anxiety and would like prayer to be more confident in walking with the Lord. As I also was suffering from anxiety, I felt this was NO coincidence! And what are the chances he came straight to me?

I've never seen this kid there before, and there was something about him I can't explain. I got chills when I held his hand. I say kid, but he probably was about mid-20s. He had a darling way of speaking like an old soul. So we all held hands and closed our eyes and prayed for him quickly, and then he paused and started praying for all of us! His prayer was so different, so beautiful! His girlfriend was in the ladies' room while we were praying. When she walked out, he introduced her to us, and she had this deep stare. Something was so different about these two.

I don't want this to sound sensationalized, but I felt such a strange energy. When I got in my car to leave, I remember thinking God did you? No, it couldn't be? But man, my heart was telling me how big God is and how not to question if he is able! I started to believe these were Angels sent by God! We got a divine appointment! Call me crazy, but I believed it! I never saw these two young kids again.

Hebrews 13:2 whispers its truth: *"Do not forget to show hospitality to strangers, for by so doing some people have shown hospitality to angels without knowing it."* Sometimes, the community extends beyond the people we know. Sometimes it includes divine appointments with strangers who might be more than they appear. Sometimes, a Panera

Bread becomes holy ground where heaven touches earth through the simple act of believers praying together.

***

I had a friend who was with me for years, "D," when our kids were little, and we were both single moms. She and I shared so much. We did a lot together. Our favorite place was Pizza Hut when you could dine in. We looked out for each other. I was so grateful for her in my life. But as we got older, and life took over, we didn't see each other as much. Not sure how it happened but there was a shift. We are still friends and love each other, and when we see each other, it's as if time hasn't passed. I love that! I love her!!

Ecclesiastes 3:1 reminds us, *"There is a time for everything, and a season for every activity under the heavens."* Some friendships are intense for a season, then gentle for a lifetime. They don't end but merely change shape. And that's okay. In fact, it is beautiful in its own way. The love remains, even when the daily presence doesn't.

I've been blessed with friends who came and never left and helped me to believe in myself. When I was younger, I was working towards a singing career, and my then Manager and his girlfriend played such a crucial part in my staying on track. Even though I got pregnant at a young age, they never once judged me or alienated me. They always encouraged me to finish school and always believed in me! He was like the Big Brother I never had, and she was like the big sister I never had. I looked up to them with respect and adoration! Till this day, we always keep in touch, and I love their example of true friendship! I know God assigned these people in my life for a reason! Friendship is a give-and-take of love! Iron sharpens Iron!!

Proverbs 27:17 says it perfectly: *"As iron sharpens iron, so one person sharpens another."* These friends didn't let me settle for less than God's best for my life. They saw potential in me when I was just a scared teenage mom. They spoke life over me when I wanted to give up. They were God's hands and feet, showing me what unconditional love looks like with skin on.

***

Friendship also comes to you in the form of sisters from another mister, that was J&J for me. We've been friends since we were teenagers. We've had ups and downs. We know so much about each other and God has kept us together for a reason! We aren't perfect, and our story has gaps for sure, but one thing that has never dissolved is our love for each other! Dysfunctional family? Maybe. But aren't the best ones full of chaos? A little, I suppose!

Life would not be the same without their love and individuality! We are all so different but there is a balance! I just imagine God writing our story and I believe what God has put together no man can separate. The enemy prowls around like a lion looking to separate and devour. Once I started to notice the attacks on these "SHIPS," I prayed harder! Still a baby in Christ, but I knew what was happening in the spirit realm! We must die to the flesh and self-righteousness! Nowhere in the Bible does it say being right unlocks the favor of God! That was my mindset. Flawed but forgiven!

For someone to know you for so many seasons of life is a gift. You can't unbox who you are in one sitting! There was a Maribel 30 years ago, and now, who I am is not the same. We grow, and we evolve! What a gift to have people in your life who know all versions of you and still love you!

Romans 12:10 instructs us to *"Be devoted to one another in love. Honor one another above yourselves."* Thirty years of friendship means thirty years of choosing each other through changes, growth, mistakes, victories, and everything in between. It means seeing each other at our worst and still believing in each other's best. That's not just friendship; that's a covenant.

***

His word says, hate what is evil and cling to what is good!

Love is patient, love is kind! It does not envy, it does not boast, it is not proud. It does not dishonor others, it is not self-seeking, it is not easily angered, it keeps no record of wrongs. 1 Corinthians 13:4–8

Boy, have I failed at that many times! I thought because in my head I was justified by being "Right"! As if God would applaud that! When people reject you or sin against you, it is a spiritual battle that demands reverent prayer! I've learned so much from the struggles and attacks of the mind. God sees our hearts.

No community is perfect because people aren't perfect. We hurt each other, disappoint each other, misunderstand each other. But Colossians 3:13 gives us the way out: *"Bear with each other and forgive one another if any of you has a grievance against someone. Forgive as the Lord forgave you."* So yes, real community requires real forgiveness, over and over again.

One who has unreliable friends soon comes to ruin, but there is a friend who sticks closer than a brother.

Proverbs 18:24

Though one may be overpowered, two can defend themselves.

A cord of three strands is not quickly broken.

Ecclesiastes 4:12

Nothing is a coincidence. God has placed people in our lives to help in our journey. I believe we get to see the ugly sometimes to know what to pray for ourselves and for others. Glory to God!

***

Looking back on times when I closed off everyone and kept myself in a closed cell to not feel, to not be disappointed to not let the world have access to me, I now know that was not from God! The church is a body. The body of Christ! All parts have a function! We must stay connected to believers and help those who are lost. I say this humbly to help those who need to allow themselves to be loved. Because there was a time I felt alone and disconnected, and didn't mind being there because the pain of letting anyone in and rejecting me would be far more to deal with.

But here's what I learned: the pain of isolation is always greater than the risk of rejection. Always. Because we were made for connection. Genesis 2:18 tells us, *"It is not good for the man to be alone."* That wasn't just about Adam needing Eve. That was about all of us needing each other. God Himself exists in community—Father, Son, and Holy Spirit. If the Trinity needs relationship, how much more do we?

***

I've had friends I've known for 30-plus years. We know our good, our bad, and our ugly! I've witnessed how God has called each one of us closer to him! It wasn't always like that. I can say for myself, I saw how the demons tried to break something so beautiful! I started calling out the demons by name! Jealousy be gone! Pride be gone! Self-righteousness be gone! Bitterness be gone! These are demons that are meant to destroy us!

If I am sick, I would love a prayer! If I need confidence, I would love a prayer! If I need doors of success, I would love a prayer! If I need a friend in action, I would love to be present! I couldn't have appreciated what I have in a friend if it weren't for God's grace and mercy! I'm imagining Abraham and God conversing! God called Abraham a friend. Can you imagine God calling you a friend!? What an honor, A friend is someone who wants to see you grow, who wants only the best for you! No hidden agendas or secrecy. There is only transparency! This gift is not from you but from God!

John 15:15 blows my mind every time I read: *"I no longer call you servants, because a servant does not know his master's business. Instead, I have called you friends, for everything that I learned from my Father I have made known to you."* Jesus calls us friends. The Creator of the universe wants friendship with us. And He models what true friendship looks like—transparent, sacrificial, eternal.

Proverbs 17:17

A friend loves at all times, and a brother is born for a time of adversity.

You must test the spirits! 1 John 4:1 Beloved, believe not every spirit, but try the spirits whether they are of God: because many false prophets are gone out into the world.

Not everyone has the same journey, not the same learning experience, or is even designed to love how you love!

***

Now, let's look at the 9 fruits of the spirit: love, joy, peace, patience, kindness, goodness, faithfulness, gentleness, and self-control.

When you find people who display these fruits, hold onto them. They're God's gift to you. And when you display these fruits, you become God's gift to someone else. That's how the body works, each part supplying what the other needs.

During the loss of my Dad, I had the company of one of my best friends! I felt so happy to have her here. She didn't need to do anything. It was just her presence that made me forget about the pain I was feeling. I could be myself, without judgments! And felt good to be heard! So imagine the HOLY Spirit, coming and keeping you company, listening to you when you need to vent or provide guidance. I'm feeling like God mirrors what friendship should look like because the Holy Spirit is with you always listening, watching, guiding and most of all loving!

Job's friends get a bad rap for their theology, but you know what they did right? They sat with him in silence for seven days (Job 2:13). Sometimes the best thing a friend can do is just be present. Without words or solutions. Just presence. That's what the ministry of presence looks like.

She always encourages me to be better or finds ways to get me to tap into my creative side. "J"

God, you are such a deets kinda guy!! Heehee.. you!

***

So many friendships, relationships I've been in that I saw the hand of God cultivate, grow, nourish, some were for a season, a reason, or a lifetime, just like the saying.

Marriage requires work; friendships require work. They are not always perfect.

1 Peter 4:8 reminds us, *"Above all, love each other deeply, because love covers over a multitude of sins."* Deep love doesn't mean perfect relationships. It means imperfect people choosing to love through the imperfections. It means showing up when it's inconvenient. It means forgiving before they ask. It means believing the best when you've seen the worst.

***

I received so much support from friends and family!

To my mentor/friend/sister in Christ, Maria Lugo, and my therapist, Shani Cephas. I know God placed you in my life for a reason, and I'm eternally grateful for your compassion and guidance.

My mentor, Maria, would call me to just offer advice on how to cope or to be mindful of taking care of myself.

Titus 2:3–4 talks about older women teaching younger women. Maria became that for me. She wouldn't simply teach me theology, but she taught me how to live it out when life falls apart. She showed me what it looks like to hold onto faith when your hands are shaking.

***

I also dearly admire my uncle, who lives in Jersey, and would call me almost every day to speak life over me. I still remember he would say: "God is NOT finished with you yet, Mari"! That gave me hope!

Sometimes family becomes your first church, your first experience of God's love with skin on. My uncle's daily calls were like daily bread, sustaining me when I couldn't feed myself spiritually.

My mom, no matter what I was feeling in my body that felt terminal, she would say, "You're going to be fine," and I believed her! It got to the point where I would call her and say Mommy please just tell me everything is gonna be ok as I wept! This happened almost every day! My Mom and my daughter were like a tower of strength for me!

One of my best friends, "J," would text me every day to check on me, to make me laugh, or to remind me she was not far, only a call, text, or drive away. I felt their love!

Galatians 6:2 tells us to *"Carry each other's burdens, and in this way you will fulfill the law of Christ."* That's what they did. They carried me. Day after day. Text after text. Call after call. They fulfilled the law of Christ by simply refusing to let me sink.

And you know what I've learned about the body of Christ? I learned that every part really does matter. The friend who texts you funny memes when you're depressed is a ministry. The one who shows up with coffee without being asked, that's the hands of Jesus. The one who listens to you ugly cry over the phone, that's the heart of God.

1 Corinthians 12:26 says, *"If one part suffers, every part suffers with it; if one part is honored, every part rejoices with it."* That's what real community does. It suffers together. It celebrates together. It refuses to let any member bear their burden alone.

I think about all the people God has placed in my life, some for moments, some for seasons, some for a lifetime. Each one left a fingerprint on my soul. Each one taught me something about God's love. Each one was a thread of His grace He's been weaving in my life.

The church is not a building. It is neither a Sunday service. It is not a denomination either. The church, in essence, is people – messy, broken, beautiful people—choosing to do life together, to bear each other's burdens, to celebrate each other's victories, to point each other back to Jesus when we lose our way.

Because "I AM" designed us for community. Because He exists in the community. Because the same God who said *"Let Us make man in Our image"* (Genesis 1:26) created us to reflect that divine community here on earth.

We need each other, not only when a crisis hits, though that's when it becomes most obvious. We need each other on ordinary Tuesday afternoons, in the small victories no one else would understand, in the fears we're afraid to speak out loud, in the dreams we're scared to pursue.

This is the beauty of the body of Christ. We don't have to be strong all the time. We can take turns. When I'm weak, you're strong. When you fall, I help you up. When neither of us can stand, someone else holds us both.

That's not a weakness, but the design. That's the body of Christ functioning exactly as it should.

Because of "I AM," we are never alone. Even when we feel alone. Even when we've built walls. Even when we're afraid to let people in. He keeps sending people to knock on our doors, to refuse to give up on us, to love us back to life.

And that, my friends, is the Gospel.

Chapter 11

Finding Purpose in Pain

There's a divine economy in the Kingdom of God that makes no earthly sense. In this economy, weakness becomes strength, loss becomes gain, even the pain that you sometimes find too unbearable to endure becomes purpose. 2 Corinthians 12:10 reveals this mystery: *"That is why, for Christ's sake, I delight in weaknesses, in insults, in hardships, in persecutions, in difficulties. For when I am weak, then I am strong."*

I didn't understand this equation for the longest time. How could weakness equal strength? How could pain equal purpose? But God's mathematics have never followed human logic. His ways are higher, His thoughts beyond ours (Isaiah 55:8–9). And in His economy, nothing, absolutely nothing, is wasted.

***

When I found out I was pregnant at sixteen, my entire world shifted. Dreams I'd been chasing suddenly felt impossibly far away.

How could I have let this happen? I was on the verge of a singing career! I had a team of people helping me realize my dreams. My stage name CARIZMA! I was performing and having fun like a teenager. I recorded an album called "ALIVE" by Maribel on Apple Music, Spotify, iTunes, and Amazon. This was a gift, but with all the other responsibilities in my life, it quickly faded, and I stored it away in a box labeled dreams for later, along with my creative abilities to DIY or make something out of nothing. My mind was always on high speed. I couldn't shut it off.

Once I had an idea to create, it was like a euphoric cloud of dopamine. I always invited God into my space as I created, asking Him to guide me, to pour into me, and I so believed it. I believed He spent all those times of writing, building, making things with me.

Ecclesiastes 3:11 whispers a profound truth: *"He has made everything beautiful in its time. He has also set eternity in the human heart; yet no one can fathom what God has done from beginning to end."* Those dreams I boxed up weren't buried; they were planted. Seeds that needed the darkness of soil, the pressure of earth, the patience of seasons before they could bloom into something greater than I ever imagined.

Years later, long after I'd become a mother and learned to navigate single parenthood, God would remind me that He was still in my creative space. He still guided and still taught.

I remember this one time I said I wanted a challenge. Be careful what you ask for! I heard the Holy Spirit tell me the next morning, *Go make a sleigh.* A Sleigh? Not a figurine or a tiny sleigh, He wanted me to make a sleigh like a big one that I could sit in. Even for me, this was on another level. I asked my uncle Ricky to drive me to Home Depot to buy some wood.

So the next couple of weeks, I'd be out in the garage by myself, cutting wood, sanding, painting, and talking to God the whole way through. My neighbors across the street were watching me every day; I'm sure they were trying to figure out what this girl was trying to build. The day had finally arrived, it was almost 8:30 pm, and I was sweating and tired, but the sleigh was complete! I literally sat on my driveway in tears cause I couldn't believe I made this. I had no experience, never built anything like this before. But I knew God helped me with every detail. He gets all the credit.

My neighbor came over and just clapped and said, "I watched you every day, and I'm so proud of you. You're amazing!" God challenged me and I did it.. I'm so in awe of His majesty!!

This sleigh was more than wood and nails. It was a parable in action. God was showing me that He could take someone with no experience, no training, no qualifications, and create something magnificent through them. Zechariah 4:6 declares, *"Not by might nor by power, but by my Spirit, says the LORD Almighty."* Every cut, every sand, every stroke of paint was a prayer. Every doubt overcome was faith in action. That sleigh stands as a monument to what God can do through willing hands and an obedient heart.

***

There's a transformation that happens in suffering. It is a mysterious alchemy where God takes the lead of our pain and transmutes it into the gold of purpose. Job understood this when he declared in Job 23:10, *"But He knows the way that I take; when He has tested me, I will come forth as gold."*

The testing isn't pleasant. The refining fire burns. But what emerges is pure, precious, powerful. Every trial I faced was removing impurities I didn't even know existed: pride, self-sufficiency, the illusion of control. What remained was faith refined, hope purified, love distilled to its essence.

Even as a young single mother, working multiple jobs and finishing school, I could see God's hand providing for me in ways I couldn't explain.

Psalm 75:6–7 reminds us, *"No one from the east or the west or from the desert can exalt themselves. It is God who judges: He brings one down, He exalts another."* Every position, every provision, every open door, they were all divine appointments. God was writing a story of provision that would become my testimony of His faithfulness.

Genesis 50:20 is the thesis statement of redemption: *"You intended to harm me, but God intended it for good to accomplish what is now being done, the saving of many lives."* Every attack of the enemy, every scheme to destroy me, God was already ten steps ahead, turning it into a setup for His glory.

This is the multiplication principle of the Kingdom. One seed dies and falls to the ground; it produces many seeds (John 12:24). My pain, when surrendered to God, becomes a harvest of healing for others. My testimony becomes someone else's breakthrough. My survival becomes someone else's hope.

***

I think of Joseph's coat of many colors, torn from him in jealousy, stained with blood, presented as evidence of his death. Yet God was weaving a greater garment of authority and redemption that would save nations. My life feels like that sometimes, like strips of different colors, some bright, some dark, some I would never have chosen. But the Master Weaver sees the pattern. He knows how each thread contributes to the masterpiece.

1 Peter 5:10 promises, *"And the God of all grace, who called you to his eternal glory in Christ, after you have suffered a little while, will himself restore you and make you strong, firm and steadfast."* Notice it says "after you have suffered." Not "if you suffer" but "after." The suffering is assumed. It's part of the process. But it's not the end of the story.

***

So who am I, beyond these trials? Who was I before the pain shaped me?

After knowing all this about me, you might wonder: Was there more to my story than suffering? Let me take you back to the beginning.

We all have a story to tell. I was born and raised in Paterson, New Jersey! I was raised in a busy house. I have one sister. We lived in my grandparents' house for most of our childhood. My story begins here! In all my dreams, my grandparents' house is my safe place!

I went to grammar school at PS 24! Made so many friends and wonderful teachers! The BEST! Mr. and Mrs. Healy, Ms. Pugatch, Ms. Chapman, Mrs. Rhein, Ms. Lauren and so many more! God really blessed me there!

Little Me was always singing, making things. Writing stories. I followed my grandfather around like a shadow, always watching him paint, lay tile, etc. I learned a lot from him. I learned all about Christmas and its glory from them, too! I'm blessed to have the parents I have for their love and presence! I always loved music and writing songs.

I loved life and all the beauty around me! I'm a hopeless romantic and loved, Love!

If I considered you a friend, it was with all my heart!

In high school, I loved fashion and always made my own way. I loved vintage and boy did that attract some kind of attention. Not sure if people were ready for that. But I was always myself! It didn't change the way I chose to express myself. You don't learn Carizma, you're born with it! I don't apologize for that! It took a long time for me to gain the confidence to say that!

As an adult, I worked in finance, real estate, human resources, selling ice cream, and even did Mary Kay at one point. I was always open to learning new things. Today I work for a top-tier accounting firm, and it's been a blessing to me and my family for many years. If I said this was my passion, that would not be true, but it allows me to contribute and still pursue the things I love.

***

There's something profound that happens when we finally understand that our lives are not random collections of events but part of a bigger story working together. Every moment, even the messy ones, plays its role in the narrative. Ephesians 2:10 reveals this truth: *"For we are God's handiwork, created in Christ Jesus to do good works, which God prepared in advance for us to do."*

The Greek word for "handiwork" is "poiema," from which we get our word "poem." We are God's poetry, His masterpiece, His magnum opus. And like any great work of art, we're not meant to be hidden away. We're meant to display His glory, to point others to the Artist.

And here's the paradox I've discovered: The very things that should have destroyed me became the things that defined me, not as a victim, but as a victor. The experiences that should have made me bitter made me better. The losses that should have emptied me actually filled me with compassion and understanding I never could have gained any other way.

Paul understood this paradox when he wrote in Philippians 3:7–8, *"But whatever were gains to me I now consider loss for the sake of Christ. What is more, I consider everything a loss because of the surpassing worth of knowing Christ Jesus my Lord, for whose sake I have lost all things."*

I lost so much along the way. I lost my childhood to a teenage pregnancy. I lost years to an abusive relationship. I lost my son Noah. I lost my father. I lost parts of myself I'll never get back. But in losing, I found. I found a God who is closer than my breath. I found a strength that wasn't my own. I found a purpose that transcends my pain.

Isaiah 61:1–3 describes the ministry Jesus claimed for Himself, and by extension, for us: *"The Spirit of the Sovereign LORD is on me, because the LORD has anointed me to proclaim good news to the poor. He has sent me to bind up the brokenhearted, to proclaim freedom for the captives and release from darkness for the prisoners... to comfort all who mourn, and provide for those who grieve in Zion—to bestow on them a crown of beauty instead of ashes."*

This is what purpose looks like when it's born from pain. It's not abstract or theoretical. It's hands that hold, tears that mingle, presence that stays when everyone else leaves. It's knowing exactly what to say, or not say, because you've been there. It's being living proof that morning comes, that joy returns, that God is faithful.

***

2 Corinthians 4:17–18 offers a perspective that changes everything: *"For our light and momentary troubles are achieving for us an eternal glory that far outweighs them all. So we fix our eyes not on what is seen, but on what is unseen, since what is seen is temporary, but what is unseen is eternal."*

Light and momentary? Some of my troubles felt anything but light. Some lasted years, not moments. But from eternity's vantage point, even our longest trials are but a breath. And they're achieving something, actively working, actively producing, an eternal glory that will make every tear worth it.

So what is the ultimate purpose of pain? It's to know Him and make Him known. It's to become so intimately acquainted with the God of all comfort that we can't help but comfort others. It's to have our faith tested and proven genuine so that it results in praise, glory, and honor when Jesus Christ is revealed (1 Peter 1:7).

My pain gave me a platform. Not one I chose, but one I've learned to steward. Every scar is a speaking point. Every wound healed is a witness. Every testimony shared is a seed planted in someone else's desert.

Revelation 12:11 says, *"They triumphed over him by the blood of the Lamb and by the word of their testimony."* Our testimonies are weapons. They're evidence that God is who He says He is, that He does what He says He'll do. They're proof that darkness doesn't win, that death doesn't have the final word, that pain always has purpose in the hands of a sovereign God.

***

So, if you're reading this in the middle of your own pain, wondering what possible purpose it could serve, let me tell you what I know for sure: God doesn't waste anything. Not a single tear. Not a single sleepless night. Not a single moment of agony. He's collecting them all, and He's preparing to transform them into something beautiful.

Your pain is not your prison; it's your preparation. Your trial is not your tombstone; it's your testimony in the making. Your mess is not your final verdict; it's your message being formed.

The same God who met me in my teenage pregnancy, who held me through abuse, who caught me when I hemorrhaged, who sustained me through loss after loss, He's the same God who is with you right now. He sees you and knows you. He has a purpose for every pain you're enduring.

The Final Declaration

My name is Maribel, but my identity is not in my name. It's not in my failures or successes. It's not in my pain or my purpose. My identity is in the "I AM" who called me, chose me, and keeps me.

Because "I AM" exists, I exist. Because "I AM" loves, I can love. Because "I AM" redeems, my pain has purpose. Because "I AM" is faithful, my story isn't over.

And neither is yours.

This is not the end. This is just the beginning of understanding that every single thing in your life, the good, the bad, the ugly, the beautiful, is all material for the masterpiece God is creating. You are not a mistake. You are not forgotten. You are not purposeless.

You are chosen and called. You are being equipped through every trial to fulfill a purpose that only you can fulfill, because only you have walked your specific path of pain.

Chapter 12

Closing Reflections & Prayer

My life was never mine; it was a story knit together and written by the finger of God. We all have a story to tell, and this has been mine, not because it's extraordinary, but because it's evidence of an extraordinary God working through an ordinary life.

When I started this journey of writing, I asked God for confirmation. Now, at the end of these pages, I see His fingerprints on every chapter, every trial, every triumph. Psalm 90:17 says, *"May the favor of the Lord our God rest on us; establish the work of our hands for us—yes, establish the work of our hands."* This book is the work of His hands through mine.

Every day, we can choose to grow and learn. We can choose to be thankful for His presence not only in the mountaintop moments but in the valleys too, where His presence is equally important. Psalm 100:4 reminds us to *"Enter his gates with thanksgiving and his courts with praise; give thanks to him and praise his name."*

These days, I don't want anything that doesn't point to Him. Every conversation or decision, I want it all to reflect His glory. Matthew 6:33 has become my compass: *"But seek first his kingdom and his righteousness, and all these things will be given to you as well."*

He humbled me when I felt at my lowest. I had nowhere to go but to Him.. Sometimes He allows us to reach the end of ourselves so we can discover the beginning of Him. 2 Chronicles 7:14 promises, *"If my people, who are called by my name, will humble themselves and pray* and seek my face and turn from their wicked ways, then I will hear from heaven, and I will forgive their sin and will heal their land." We are here for such a short while, James 4:14 calls our life *"a mist that appears for a little while and then vanishes"* so I plan to give all of me until He calls me home. Every breath, every heartbeat, every moment is an opportunity to glorify Him.

***

Corinthians 1:3–4 : *"Praise be to the God and Father of our Lord Jesus Christ, the Father of compassion and the God of all comfort, who comforts us in all our troubles, so that we can comfort those in any trouble with the comfort we ourselves receive from God."* Your pain is not the end of your story; it's the beginning of your ministry. Every scar you carry is a testimony someone else needs to hear. Every victory you've won is proof for someone still fighting.

When I think of it, I'm filled with emotions of how good God is! Psalm 34:8 invites us to *"Taste and see that the Lord is good; blessed is the one who takes refuge in him."* I've tasted His goodness in the bitter seasons. I've seen His faithfulness in the darkest nights. I can talk all day long about the hand of God in my life. There have been so many times He's revealed Himself, in the obvious miracles and in the quiet whispers, in the dramatic rescues and in the daily provisions. Lamentations 3:22–23 has become my morning anthem: *"Because of the Lord's great love we are not consumed, for his compassions never fail. They are new every morning; great is your faithfulness."*

Yes, it is an amazing feeling to think that the King of the Universe loves me, He sent His Son to die for me, and He knows me by name! Isaiah 43:1 declares this intimate truth: *"Fear not, for I have redeemed you; I have summoned you by name; you are mine."* Not just one of billions, but known, called, chosen by name. Your name is written on His hands (Isaiah 49:16). Your tears are collected in His bottle (Psalm 56:8). Your days were written in His book before one of them came to be (Psalm 139:16).

Isn't it incredible how everything points to Him? My gifts are not mine; they are from the Lord for His glory! My dreams, they are not mine; they are from the Lord! 1 Corinthians 4:7 asks, *"What do you have that you did not receive? And if you did receive it, why do you boast as though you did not?"* The circle He has placed me in was carefully designed, from family to friends to Sisters in Christ Bible studies to coworkers to even strangers I've met disguised as angels. Nothing is random. Proverbs 16:9 reminds us, *"In their hearts humans plan their course, but the Lord establishes their steps."*

A Legacy of Hope

I hope this book conveys hope, healing, and inspiration. You are never alone! Deuteronomy 31:8 promises, *"The Lord himself goes before you and will be with you; he will never leave you nor forsake you. Do not be afraid; do not be discouraged."* We are all beautifully defined by His very hand! You are not an accident. You are not a mistake. You are God's workmanship, His poetry, His masterpiece. And He's not finished with you yet.

"Because 'I AM'… that is what I heard in my spirit!" Because God never left me! The Holy Spirit would speak to me and keep me focused. Not by my might at all! This echoes Zechariah 4:6: *"Not by might nor by power, but by my Spirit,' says the Lord Almighty."* The sickness I feel in my body serves as a reminder to keep thriving and keep declaring His promises for my life. Even Paul had his thorn in the flesh, and God told him, *"My grace is sufficient for you, for my power is made perfect in weakness"* (2 Corinthians 12:9).

***

When I visualize a garden, I see my grandma's house in the middle, because somehow that is my safe place in my dreams. Psalm 91:1–2 says, *"Whoever dwells in the shelter of the Most High will rest in the shadow of the Almighty. I will say of the Lord, 'He is my refuge and my fortress, my God, in whom I trust.'"* Some of the things I see in my grandfather, uncles, and Dad growing up are the grand opening to hearing God's voice. They are all wrapped up into my Creator. He gave me parts of Himself in these people in my life as a small picture of who He is: Loving, Caring, Funny, Provider, Protector!

And you know what? I love rainbows as they're God's promise painted across the sky. Beautiful skies that declare His glory. Old movies that remind me simpler times still held complex faith. Hearing testimonies that prove God is still moving. Sharing the word as it presents itself, not forced but flowing naturally like rivers of living water. Because I absolutely love humor and I picture God as this funny guy who just makes me laugh, and I'm not afraid to be myself with Him. Proverbs 17:22 tells us, *"A cheerful heart is good medicine,"* and I believe our God delights in our joy.

And we are all beautifully defined by His very hand! Psalm 139:14 declares, *"I praise you because I am fearfully and wonderfully made; your works are wonderful, I know that full well."* Romans 8:38–39 has become my foundation: *"For I am convinced that neither death nor life, neither angels nor demons, neither the present nor the future, nor any powers, neither height nor depth, nor anything else in all creation, will be able to separate us from the love of God that is in Christ Jesus our Lord."*

"The fruit of healing from the wounds of the past, is using what you went through, to help other people" - Maribel

Epilogue

The Journey Continues

Dear beloved reader,

As I close this book, I want you to know that the ending of these pages is not the ending of the story, neither mine nor yours. Life continues to unfold, faith continues to grow, and God continues to work. What you've read is simply a snapshot of an ongoing journey, a testimony still being written, a faith still being refined. I'm not perfect, I fail all the time and fall short of His glory, I'm still working through not feeling well at times, and the inevitable aging pains, but GOD! This body may fail but my spirit and soul sing His praises every day! I rely on his promises, and when this body is ready to lie at rest, I'm confident in knowing God is with me! To be absent in the body is to be present in the Lord! What a gift to look forward to! Nothing sad about that!

I wanted to leave something my kids and grandkids could be proud of!

The best thing you could ever be is simply YOURSELF unapologetically! Some of this book has areas of my life I've never shared and wanted to reassure them. They are never alone, and they are adored beyond their understanding. I honestly feel like the richest girl in the world! God blessed me with a wonderful life full of wonder, full of growth!

If you've made it this far, you've walked with me through valleys and mountaintops, through tears and laughter, through death and life. You've seen that faith isn't about having all the answers. Rather, it is about knowing the One who does. Your story is still being written. Your pain is not your conclusion. Your mistakes are not your identity. Your struggles are not your destiny. The same "I AM" who carried me is ready to carry you. The same God who turned my ashes into beauty wants to do the same for you. The same Jesus who gave me purpose in my pain is waiting to reveal purpose in yours.

Philippians 1:6 promises us, *"Being confident of this, that he who began a good work in you will carry it on to completion until the day of Christ Jesus."* The God who started your story isn't finished with you yet. He's still writing, still working, still weaving beauty from brokenness.

So, if you're reading this in a season of waiting, wondering when your breakthrough will come and when your pain will finally make sense, let me remind you of something I've learned through every trial: God's timing is perfect, even when it feels perfectly wrong to us.

Ecclesiastes 3:11 tells us, *"He has made everything beautiful in its time."* Not in our time. Not when we demand it. Not when we think we're ready. But in His time, the perfect time that considers every thread in the tapestry, every note in the symphony, every person who will be touched by your story.

I waited years to understand why certain things happened. Some things I'm still waiting to understand. But I've learned that waiting is not wasted time when you're waiting on the Lord. Isaiah 40:31 promises, *"But those who hope in the Lord will renew their strength. They will soar on wings like eagles; they will run and not grow weary, they will walk and not be faint."*

Every tear you've cried has been collected.

Every prayer you've whispered has been heard.

Every broken piece of your heart is known to the God who specializes in restoration. Your pain is not pointless. It is *preparatory*. Your struggles are not senseless. In fact, they're shaping you for something greater.

You may not see it yet. You may not feel it yet. But God is working. He's always working. Romans 8:28 isn't a platitude but a promise: *"And we know that in all things God works for the good of those who love him, who have been called according to his purpose."*

Jeremiah 29:11 has become more than a verse to me. It's become a lifeline: *"'For I know the plans I have for you,' declares the Lord, 'plans to prosper you and not to harm you, plans to give you hope and a future.'"*

These plans aren't always easy, and they may not always make sense. Sometimes they lead through valleys so dark you can't even see your next step. But they always lead somewhere. They always have a purpose. They always end in His glory and your good.

Your life is not a series of random events or chaos without meaning. Every single thing, every joy, every sorrow, every victory, every defeat is being woven into a masterpiece by the Master Weaver who sees the full picture even when you can only see threads.

***

Jesus promised us in John 14:27, *"Peace I leave with you; my peace I give you. I do not give to you as the world gives. Do not let your hearts be troubled and do not be afraid."*

This peace doesn't mean the absence of storms; instead, it is His presence in the storm. It doesn't mean everything makes sense but trusting the One who makes sense of everything. It doesn't mean you won't cry. It means you're never crying alone.

The peace God offers transcends understanding (Philippians 4:7). It guards our hearts and minds even when our circumstances scream that we should panic.

It's the peace I found in a hospital room holding my dying father's hand.

It's the peace that came after losing Noah.

It's the peace that sustained me through abuse, divorce, and medical trauma.

It's supernatural, unexplainable,

***

Above all, I want you to know that *YOU ARE LOVED*. Not in a general, vague way. Not as one of billions. You are specifically, intentionally, passionately loved by the God who created the universe.

Romans 8:35-39 asks, *"Who shall separate us from the love of Christ? Shall trouble or hardship or persecution or famine or nakedness or danger or sword?... No, in all these things we are more than conquerors through him who loved us. For I am convinced that neither death nor life, neither angels nor demons, neither the present nor the future, nor any powers, neither height nor depth, nor anything else in all creation, will be able to separate us from the love of God that is in Christ Jesus our Lord."*

Nothing. Absolutely nothing can separate you from His love. Not your mistakes. Not your doubts. Not your failures. Not your pain. Not your questions. Nothing.

Galatians 6:9 urges us, *"Let us not become weary in doing good, for at the proper time we will reap a harvest if we do not give up."*

So trust me when I tell you NEVER to give up. I know you're tired. I know you're hurting. I know some days it takes everything you have just to get out of bed. But don't give up. Your harvest is coming. Your breakthrough is approaching. Your testimony is being written.

Hebrews 12:1-2 gives us the strategy: *"Therefore, since we are surrounded by such a great cloud of witnesses, let us throw off everything that hinders and the sin that so easily entangles. And let us run with perseverance the race marked out for us, fixing our eyes on Jesus, the pioneer and perfecter of faith."*

You're not running alone. You are surrounded by witnesses who've gone before and those who've overcome, and also those who are cheering you on. And most importantly, Jesus Himself is both your example and your strength.

Your Story Matters

Your story, with all its messiness, all its imperfections, all its pain, matters. It matters to God who is writing it. It matters to the people who NEED to hear it. It matters to the generations who will come after you.

You might think you're too broken to be used, too wounded to help others, too ordinary to make a difference. But God specializes in using the unlikely. He chose Moses, who stuttered; David, who was the youngest; Mary, who was a teenager; Peter, who denied Him; and Paul, who persecuted Christians. He chose me, a teen mom, an abuse survivor, a woman who's buried a child and a father, who's battled anxiety and medical trauma.

And He chooses you.

1 Corinthians 1:27-29 explains why: *"But God chose the foolish things of the world to shame the wise; God chose the weak things of the world to shame the strong. God chose the lowly things of this world and the despised things—and the things that are not—to nullify the things that are, so that no one may boast before him."*

Your weakness is the perfect canvas for His strength. Your brokenness is the perfect vessel for His healing. Your story, no matter how shattered it seems, is the perfect testimony of His redemption.

So, keep walking. As you close this book and step back into your life, remember: the journey continues. Faith is not a destination you arrive at but a daily decision to trust, to believe, to keep walking even when the path is unclear.

Some days will be harder than others. Some seasons will test everything you believe. Some moments will bring you to your knees. But in all of it, through all of it, He is there. He is faithful. He is working.

Isaiah 30:21 promises, *"Whether you turn to the right or to the left, your ears will hear a voice behind you, saying, 'This is the way; walk in it.'"*

Listen for His voice. It might come through a friend's encouragement, a scripture that suddenly comes alive, a sunset that takes your breath away, or a peace that makes no sense. He's always speaking. We just need to tune our hearts to hear.

***

A Prayer for Your Journey

Heavenly Father,

I pray a blessing over every reader of the story you wrote out for me long ago. May they see you and the hand that provides and guides. May they hear your voice and walk in the direction of your glory! If there is a dream yet unfulfilled, may they walk fearless and confident, may they find rest and renewal even as they press forward. If there is pain hidden, may their trust in you grow! Show them that their best Chapters are yet to come, that You who began a good work in them will complete it.

Thank You for the privilege of sharing my story. Thank You for every reader who saw themselves in these pages. Thank You for the testimonies that will come from their lives—stories of redemption, restoration, and revival.

We trust Your timing, perfect and purposeful. We trust Your plans, good and glorious. We trust Your love, endless and unconditional.

In Jesus' name, Amen.

One Final Promise

As you continue your journey, carry this promise with you. It's from Isaiah 41:10, and it has carried me through every storm:

"So do not fear, for I am with you; do not be dismayed, for I am your God. I will strengthen you and help you; I will uphold you with my righteous right hand."

He is with you. Right now. In this moment. In your questioning. In your doubting. In your struggling. In your hoping. He is with you.

The great "I AM" who was, who is, and who is to come – He is with you.

Your journey continues, but you don't walk it alone. You never have. You never will.

Keep walking, beloved. Keep believing. Keep hoping. Keep trusting.

And one day, when you stand before Him, you'll understand it all. Every tear. Every trial. Every triumph. You'll see how He used it all, every single piece, to create something beautiful and eternal that brought Him glory and brought others hope.

Until that day, persevere. Press on. Don't give up.

Because "I AM" is with you. Because "I AM" is for you.

Because "I AM" will never leave you nor forsake you.

And that, beloved, is enough. It has always been enough. It will always be enough.

Grace and peace to you on your continuing journey,

Maribel.

"May the God of hope fill you with all joy and peace as you trust in him, so that you may overflow with hope by the power of the Holy Spirit." —Romans 15:13

The Beginning..

www.ingramcontent.com/pod-product-compliance
Lightning Source LLC
Chambersburg PA
CBHW020740130626
46554CB00006B/2078